# COLORADO HIKING WITH KIDS

## 50 Hiking Adventures for Families

By

**Bridge Press**

**Bridge Press**
Support@BridgePress.org

ISBN: 978-1-955149-33-4

# FREE BONUS

Find Out 31 Incredible Places You Can Visit Next! Just Go To:

**purplelink.org/travel**

# TABLE OF CONTENTS

# INTRODUCTION:
# HIKING WITH KIDS

Welcome to the Colorado edition of *Hiking with Kids*! With this comprehensive hiking guide, you will have all the information you'll need to go hiking with your kids. We have outlined the 50 best hikes for hiking with kids of all ages.

For each hike, you will learn what to expect, how to get there, what you will need, and the level of difficulty. Plus, we have included a map of each hike and space to discuss what you saw while you were out enjoying the wilderness of Colorado.

**Tips for Hiking with Kids:**
Hiking with your kids is going to look a little different than just hiking with your partner. In fact, there's going to be a lot of planning involved, especially when you're first getting started. However, the planning is well worth it and can make the hiking trip a lot more fun. With these expert tips, you can plan the perfect hike with ease.

**Pack Snacks**
Especially for younger children, packing snacks is one of the most important things you can do. No one wants to be hungry on a hike, especially if it's a long one. So, you can pack some snacks to make sure that everyone is feeling energized and happy while they're hiking. It's best to bring a variety of snacks just in case you have a picky eater in your group. Some popular snacks that usually go over well on a hike include:
- Granola bars
- Crackers
- Fruit

- Sandwiches
- Fruit snacks

## Bring a Friend

If you have older children, such as elementary– or middle school–aged kids, you may have the option to bring a friend. While not all parents want to have the responsibility of bringing another child on a hike, it can be a fun experience for your kid. You might have friends with children of similar ages to yours. If so, you can all go hiking together, and it can be a huge, fun family and friend event.

## How to Plan a Bathroom Break

Not all hikes will have bathroom stations. That being said, it's important to plan your bathroom breaks before you start your hike. In this guide, we will let you know if there is currently a bathroom station at a trailhead or not.

Luckily, many of the family-friendly hikes will have a bathroom at the start of the trail. However, you may need to either stop at a gas station before you go for your hike or plan to change any diapers before you start your hike. You should dispose of any diapers in a trash bin at the trailhead since bins may be scarce along the route. All in all, plan ahead.

## Dress for Success

Layers will be your best friend. In Colorado, the weather can be unpredictable. Even if the weather is nice in Denver, it may be chilly in the mountains. Additionally, the weather can start off sunny and warm, but it can change quickly if the sun goes behind a cloud or if weather rolls in. So, you will want to bring multiple layers of clothing.

For the most part, your children can wear leggings or long pants with a T-shirt and a sweatshirt or jacket over top. If you're hiking in the summer, you want to start off with a sweatshirt on in the morning and switch to a light T-shirt or tank top in the afternoon. If you're hiking in the spring or fall, the weather can be colder, so you want to plan ahead and wear a heavier jacket.

## Active Shoes

You should wear shoes that are meant for activity. Even though many of the family-friendly trails in Colorado are paved or at least have a distinguished path, some trails can get muddy, especially if you're planning on hiking near a river or lake. So, make sure you wear tennis shoes, hiking shoes, or shoes meant for activity. Try to avoid sandals or anything with a high heel because you might end up with blisters, and that's something you'll want to avoid.

## Frequent Stops

When you're hiking with kids, you need to keep in mind that they need to make more stops than you would. If you are coming to Colorado from out of state, you also need to remember that the elevation change can take a huge toll on your body. That being said, you should plan to take a break every half a mile or so. With younger kiddos, you may even need to take a break every quarter mile. Even if your kids aren't ready to take a break yet, you should stop and at least drink some water and offer them a snack.

## Lots of Water and Fluids

Although you should be drinking on every hike that you go on, Colorado is a very dry state. Even if you aren't hiking in Colorado, you need to make sure you're drinking a lot of water so that you stay hydrated.

When you're on your hike, you'll want to make sure that every person in your party has their own water bottle. That way, you can make sure that everyone is drinking enough water. On a hot day, you definitely don't want to be caught in a situation where you don't have enough water. You could get dehydrated and feel ill.

## Make it Fun: Games to Play While Hiking

You want the hike to be fun, so you should play some games while you're hiking in the forest, sand dunes, around a lake, or wherever you end up. Some fun games that you can play on pretty much every hike include:

- Follow the Leader
- I Spy
- Having a scavenger hunt
- Searching for signs of wildlife

**Tips for Hiking with Infants, Toddlers, and Preschoolers**
When you're hiking with very young children, your best bet is to keep your hikes short. If you're hiking with infants, you may want to choose a trail that has a paved path or one that is easy enough for a stroller to roll on.

In this guide, we will let you know when the trails are paved and if they're good for younger children. You will also want to choose a time in the day when the weather is nice. Of course, you'll always want to have good weather when you're hiking, but it is especially important if you're hiking with young kids.

**Tips for Hiking with Elementary School Children**
When you're hiking with elementary school–age children, you can choose slightly harder hikes than when you're hiking with children under seven. Your elementary school–age children are likely to become more interested in wildlife over time. They may want to help you find traces of wildlife by looking for skat, tracks, or any other signs that animals were in the area. For example, you can start to teach your children about the local birds, look for the different kinds of wildflowers, or start to distinguish the different kinds of animal tracks.

**Tips for Hiking with Middle Schoolers**
Middle school–age children can handle more intense hikes. However, you still don't want to plan a very long, intense hike with a child of this

age. When you get towards the end of middle school, you can maybe try some of those more intense hikes, but you'll still want to keep your hikes easy to moderate.

When hiking with middle schoolers, you may want to choose a hike that ends in a cool overlook or has some awesome scenery along the way. Middle schoolers will likely be just as interested in an intended destination as the wildlife in the area.

## Hike Often
If you want to foster a love for the outdoors and hiking in your children, then you should hike together often. The more times you go out hiking with your kids, the better you'll get at hiking with your children. Your family will start to enjoy hiking together. So, the more you hike, the better your hiking trips with your kids will be!

## What to Bring
When you're out hiking, there are some things that you will want to bring. While it would be nice to bring pretty much everything you could possibly think of, you don't want to make your backpack too heavy.

It might be best to find either travel-sized versions of some of these items or have some of your older kids carry their own backpacks. If you have your older kids carrying their own stuff, they may also feel like they're contributing more to the hike. Here is a list of some things that you might consider bringing on a hike in Colorado:
- Jacket
- Hiking shoes
- Hat
- Sunglasses
- Sunscreen
- Water bottle
- Snacks
- Camera

- Binoculars
- Small first aid kit
- Hiking poles
- Map of the hike (sometimes offered at the trailhead, but may need to be printed at home)

**Best Hikes Breakdown**

To make choosing your hikes easier, we have separated the hikes into different groups. That way, you can choose a hike that best suits your needs and location. Instead of the hikes being a mystery in terms of what you'll see along the way, we'll let you know all of the details! Simply look at the table of contents to see which hikes feature distinct landmarks and physical characteristics. You can also go directly to the chapter that highlights specific features in Colorado, such as mountains, lakes, or sand dunes.

**Hike Difficulty Ratings**

To make it easier to figure out which hikes you want to take with your kids, we've created a rating scale that will rate each hike on its difficulty. In each section of this book, we will start out with the easiest hikes and then present the ones that are slightly more difficult. We have rated the hikes on a scale of 1 to 5, with 1 being the easiest hikes and 5 being the more difficult types.

- **1, very easy:** little elevation, good for young children
- **2, easy:** good for older preschool and elementary children
- **3, moderate**: good for older elementary and middle school
- **4, moderate to hard**: save for older middle school children
- **5, hard:** appropriate for older middle schoolers who hike often, and high schoolers

# ABOUT COLORADO

Also known as the Centennial State, Colorado became the 38th state of the United States in 1876. Colorado has a rich history of Native American culture, agriculture, ranch life, and the deserted ghost towns of the homesteaders who came to the state in search of gold, silver, and other riches.

Denver, the capital city of Colorado, is exactly one mile above sea level. That's why it's commonly referred to as the "Mile High city." If you are staying in Denver, you are exactly 5,280 feet above sea level. This is also why it's important to stay hydrated while you are visiting Colorado. If you're coming from a state that is at sea level, the elevation can really have an impact on your body.

Colorado is known for its many outdoor activities, such as hiking, camping, white water rafting, backpacking, mountain biking, wildlife watching, and more. In fact, Colorado is ranked as one of the highest, if not the highest, states that have the most physically active population of residents.

Native Colorado residents love the outdoors and take pride in their many spectacular hiking trails and camping areas. Whether you are visiting the family-oriented Estes Park or going deep into the mountains to visit an old mountain town, you are bound to find some of the most amazing outdoor activities in all the United States.

The Royal Gorge Bridge in Cañon City is actually the highest suspension bridge in the entire world. The bridge reaches a height of 1,053 feet and offers some of the most amazing views of the gorge below. There are many hikes to do near the Royal Gorge Bridge, so look for those as we get into our guide.

Some common animals that you will often come across in Colorado include deer, bighorn sheep, coyotes, prairie dogs, bears, elk, moose, and even mountain lions. See if you can find tracks, skat, or spot any of the animals while you're hiking.

# LANDSCAPE AND CLIMATE

Colorado is a mountain state. In fact, it has some of the highest mountains in the entire Continental Divide. Because of its mountains, the average altitude of the state of Colorado is 6,800 feet above sea level. Colorado has 59 mountains that are 14,000 feet or higher, and it has just about 830 mountains that are between 11,000 and 14,000 feet in elevation.

Even though Colorado is known for the Rocky Mountains, nearly 40% of the entire state is actually eastern High Plains. The High Plains in Colorado start at the border and then slope upward for about 200 miles until they get to the foothills of the Rocky Mountains.

As a headwater state, all the rivers in Colorado flow outward. The only exception is the Green River, which flows diagonally through the northwestern corner of Colorado. In fact, four of the major rivers in the United States have their original source in Colorado. These major rivers are the Colorado River, the Rio Grande, the Arkansas River, and the Platte River.

Because of the high elevation and the fact that Colorado sits in the middle of the United States, the climate is generally cool and dry compared to other parts of the U.S. However, Colorado does have distinct seasons. The summers are generally hot and can reach 100 degrees on some days, and the winters are cold and snowy, making them popular for many snow sports, such as downhill skiing, cross country skiing, and snowshoeing. Yet, it is not uncommon to have a warm 70-degree day in the middle of winter.

While the plains are generally hot, the mountains will stay cooler year round because they are at higher elevations. However, these higher elevations also mean that if you are skiing in the mountains during the wintertime, you may still get a sunburn because you are closer to the atmosphere. So, regardless of the time of year, you will always want to wear sunscreen when you are outdoors in Colorado.

# ALDERFER THREE SISTERS TRAIL (EVERGREEN)

The Alderfer Three Sisters Trail in Evergreen is a 6.6-mile loop trail with some elevation gain. This intermediate trail is a great option for your older kids and leads to a spectacular lookout to see Evergreen Mountain. You don't have to do the entire trail to get to the overlook; you can find it after just about a mile and a half of hiking. Along the way, you'll encounter beautiful forested landscapes and rocky surfaces.

**Hike Difficulty Rating:** 4

**Best Time to Visit:**
While the summertime is the best time to visit for hiking, the fall is a great time to hike because you can see the changing of the leaves.

**Pass/Permit/Fees:**
There are no passes, permits, or fees.

**How to Get There:**
From Evergreen, you'll go on Buffalo Park Road from County Highway 73. Travel just about one mile and you'll find the trailhead at Evergreen Lakehouse. There are plenty of other trails in the area, but look for Evergreen Mountain Trail east to Summit Trail.

**What to Pack:**
There is a parking area and bathrooms near the beginning of the trail. Because this trail has some elevation gain, make sure that you have good shoes and water.

**Can You Find?**
There are plenty of wildflowers along this trail, so keep your eyes out!

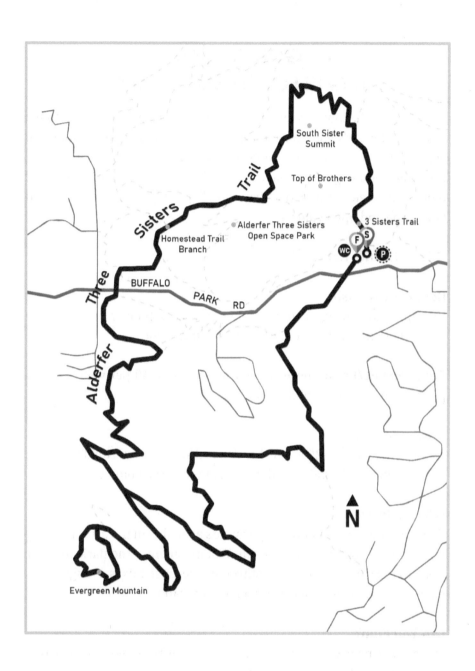

# GOULD LOOP
# (STATE FOREST STATE PARK)

Although Gould Loop is a longer trail at 6.1 miles, this loop is relatively easy to follow. It's good for families who have elementary school–age children but want to go on a long afternoon hike. When you hike along this trail, you'll go by a lake and will get to see many different mountain peaks. Along the way, you'll pass through the forested landscape and open valleys.

**Hike Difficulty Rating:** 3

**Best Time to Visit:**
Visit this trail during the midsummer months of June or July. If you go too early in the spring, you will still encounter snow.

**Pass/Permit/Fees:** There is an entrance fee of $9 per vehicle or $4 per person for a non-vehicle entry.

**How to Get There:**
From Denver, take I-25 N and 14 W to Jackson County. You'll be on the road for about 140 miles, and it takes about three hours to get there.

**What to Pack:**
There are bathrooms and campgrounds available in the area, but they might not be right at the trailhead. When you enter the park, look for signs to the campgrounds or bathrooms. Because this is a longer trail, make sure you bring snacks and plenty of water.

**Can You Find?**
Moose have been commonly spotted along this trail. See if you can find their tracks or even a moose itself.

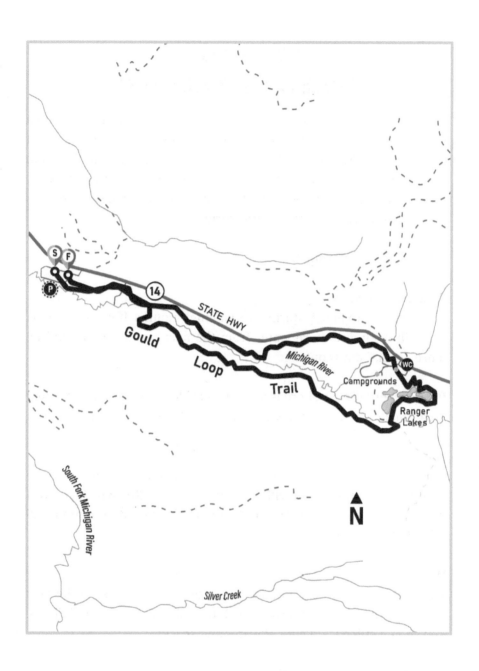

# BOBCAT TRAIL
# (RIFLE FALLS STATE PARK)

The Bobcat Trail in Rifle State Park is a popular trail that features waterfalls, limestone caves, beautiful wildflowers, fishing spots, and picnic areas. The 2.7-mile trail is popular due to the stunning Rifle Falls and because of how close you can get to the limestone caves. Bobcat Trail also has the largest rainbow trout hatchery, the Rifle Creek Fish Hatchery, in the entire world.

**Hike Difficulty Rating: 3**

**Best Time to Visit:**
The best time to hike is during the summer months. If you go in June, you will likely see more water from the falls because there will be more water from snowmelt.

**Pass/Permit/Fees:** There is a $15 vehicle fee to park in the parking area. Smaller fees may apply depending on the time of year.

**How to Get There:**
From Olathe, go east on Falcon Rd. for just about four miles. When the road turns to gravel, you will be on Peach Valley Rd., which you will continue on for 3.4 miles. Turn right on to Bobcat Rd. and continue 1.5 miles to the trailhead.

**What to Pack:**
The trails are well defined and have gravel. You can reach the falls from the Coyote Trail, which is much friendlier for younger children. You should still pack plenty of water and snacks.

**Can You Find?**
Look for wildflowers along the trail and rainbow trout as you pass by the rivers and the falls.

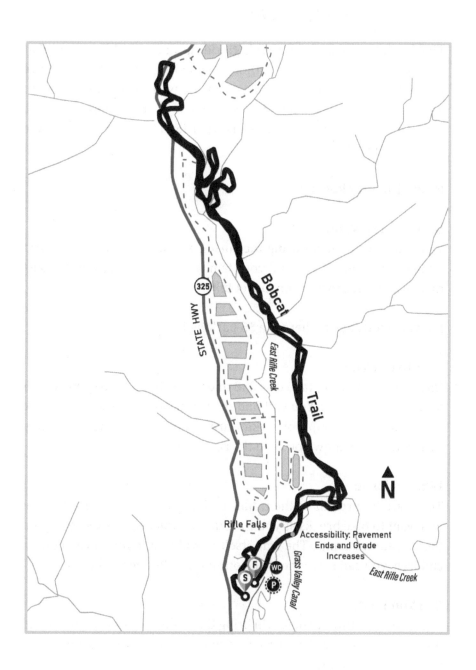

# ST. MARY'S GLACIER

The 2.4-mile trail at Saint Mary's glacier is an out-and-back trail that takes you up to the glacier. Although you are going uphill the entire first half of the trail, the views at the top are well worth it. You'll get to a glacial lake as well as Saint Mary's glacier. If you continue up the trail, you can even sit on top of Saint Mary's glacier as you look out over the mountainous peaks.

**Hike Difficulty Rating:** 3

**Best Time to Visit:**
You will want to visit during the spring, summer, or fall for the best hiking conditions. If you and your family are feeling up to it, it's best to take an early morning or sunset hike.

**Pass/Permit/Fees:** There is a $5 parking fee.

**How to Get There:**
Once you get to I-70, take exit 238 and go north on County Road 275 for about nine miles. You will find the trailhead on the left side of the road. There are a couple of parking areas, and you will likely see many cars letting you know you're in the right place.

**What to Pack:**
There are bathrooms at the trailhead. Pack a picnic for this one. You will want to take breaks as you walk up the trail because there is quite the elevation change. The trail itself is wide, so if you have younger children, you can carry them on your back or let them hike.

**Can You Find?**
In the summertime, people will bring their snowboards or skis to ride down the glacier. See if you can find some of these people skiing in the middle of the summer.

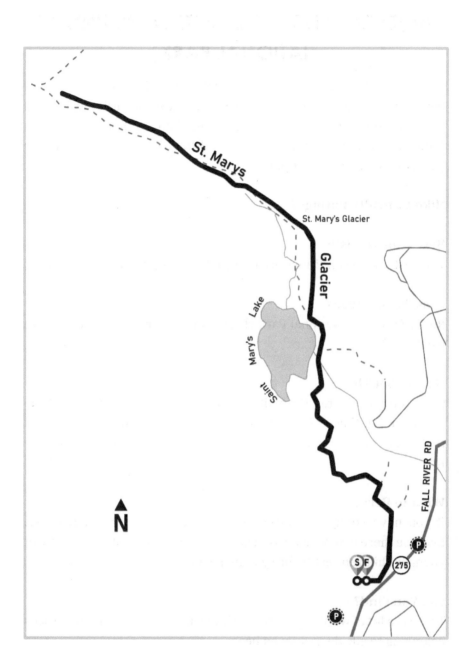

# ALBERTA FALLS TRAIL (ROCKY MOUNTAIN NATIONAL PARK)

The Alberta Falls Trail is a 1.6-mile out-and-back trail close to Estes Park. This is a family-friendly hike that features beautiful waterfalls, views of the mountain peaks, and the famous Rocky Mountain National Park. In fact, this trail is one of the most scenic hikes in the entire park and is very popular.

**Hike Difficulty Rating:** 2

**Best Time to Visit:**
The best hiking conditions are in the late spring, summer, and fall.

**Pass/Permit/Fees:**
Rocky Mountain National Park charges an entrance fee for the entire week.

**How to Get There:**
Once you are in Estes, the trailhead is 10 minutes from the Bear Lake parking lot at Glacier Gorge Junction. You will find the trailhead near the Gorge Junction parking area, which is 8.5 miles down Bear Lake Rd.

**What to Pack:**
If you have younger children, you should pack snacks and water. Because there is some elevation gain, make sure you take breaks to let younger children rest before you make it all the way up the trail.

**Can You Find?**
There is a lot of wildlife in Estes Park. See if you can find animal tracks belonging to elk, deer, or even bears.

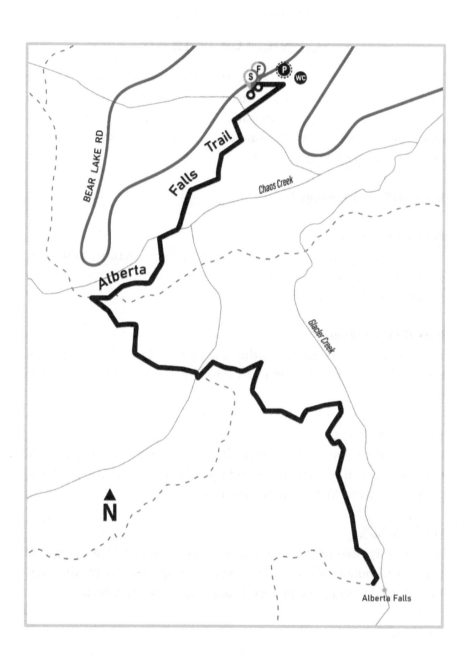

# MAROON BELLS
# SCENIC LOOP TRAIL

The scenic loop around the Maroon Bells mountains is a great hike for young children because the hike itself is short and there is not as much elevation gain as some of Colorado's other mountain hikes. On this hike, you'll pass by a beautiful mountain lake and be surrounded by mountainous peaks the entire time.

**Hike Difficulty Rating:** 2

**Best Time to Visit:**
The best hiking times are generally from May until October. However, during the spring, the trails may be muddy or still have snow, so summer or fall hiking is best.

**Pass/Permit/Fees:**
A permit is required to access the area by vehicle. Make sure to visit the area's recreation website or forest service webpage to get your permit.

**How to Get There:**
From Denver, follow I-70 towards CO-82 E in Glenwood Springs. You'll take exit 116 off of I-70 W. To find the trail, continue on CO-82 E to your destination. You will drive about 50 miles.

**What to Pack:**
As with any hike in the mountains, make sure you bring plenty of water and potentially a picnic lunch to stop and eat by the lake. Restrooms are available in the day use areas near Maroon Lake.

**Can You Find?**
Try taking this hike in the fall so that you can look for the changing colors of the leaves. What colors do you see?

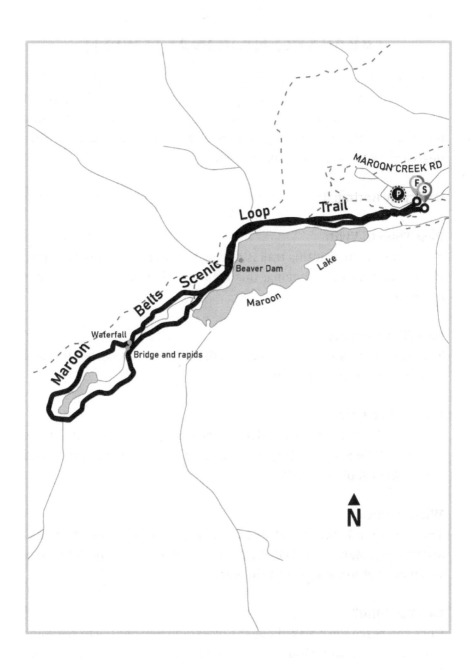

# CHIEF MOUNTAIN TRAIL (ARAPAHO NATIONAL FOREST)

The Chief Mountain Trail takes you on a beautiful 2.8-mile hike through the Rocky Mountains. As you hike through the pine trees of the Arapaho National Forest, you will get views of the stunning mountain peaks. At the end, you'll be above the trees and get a 360-degree view of the mountains as well.

**Difficulty Rating:** 3

**Best Time to Visit:**
The best time to visit this trail is during the summer and fall months. If you are into snowshoeing, this trail can also be good for winter activities.

**Pass/Permit/Fees:**
There are no fees required to park at the trailhead. However, the area is generally heavily traveled.

**How to Get There:**
To get to the trailhead from Idaho Springs, exit I-70 in Idaho Springs at exit 240. Go South on Highway 103, and you will find the trailhead five miles east of Echo Lake.

**What to Pack:**
There is not a bathroom at this trailhead, so plan bathroom breaks accordingly. Make sure to bring plenty of water and a snack to enjoy when you get to the top of the lookout.

**Can You Find?**
Once you reach the break above the trees, you will be able to see some of Colorado's most famous peaks. Can you spot Pikes Peak and Longs Peak?

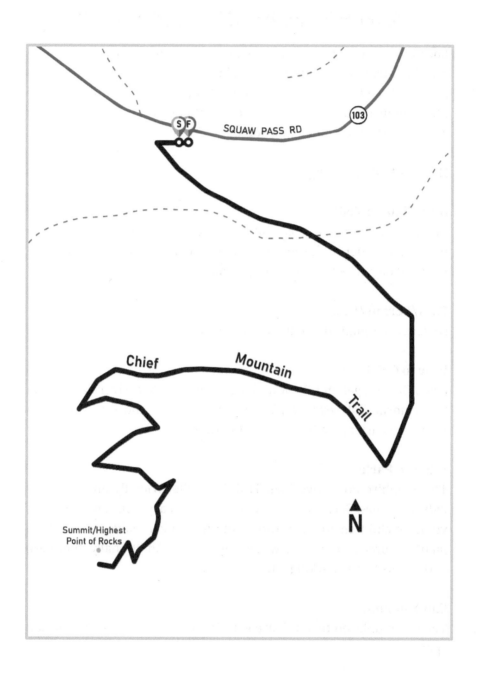

# SAPPHIRE POINT OVERLOOK TRAIL

Located near Frisco, the Sapphire Point Overlook Trail is an easy 0.6-mile loop that goes around a lake. The trail itself is packed dirt and is at least three feet wide at all points. At the end of the trail, there are plenty of picnic tables that you and your family can enjoy as you look around at the mountains that surround Frisco.

**Hike Difficulty Rating:** 1

**Best Time to Visit:**
The best time to visit this trail is May through September. Keep in mind that earlier in the summer the trail may be muddier, and there may still be packed snow on the ground.

**Pass/Permit/Fees:**
No fees are required to park at the trail and hike.

**How to Get There:**
From Denver, get on I-70 W and head towards Blue River Parkway in Silverthorne. Take exit 205, then follow US-6 East and Swan Mountain Rd. to the parking lot that marks the trailhead.

**What to Pack:**
The Sapphire Point Overlook Trail is stroller friendly and great for kids of all ages. Because the loop is short and easy, you can bring your younger children for a beautiful outdoor hike. Make sure to take plenty of breaks and bring water and snacks. Additionally, there are bathrooms by the parking lot.

**Can You Find?**
The chipmunks on this trail are very friendly. See how many you can spot!

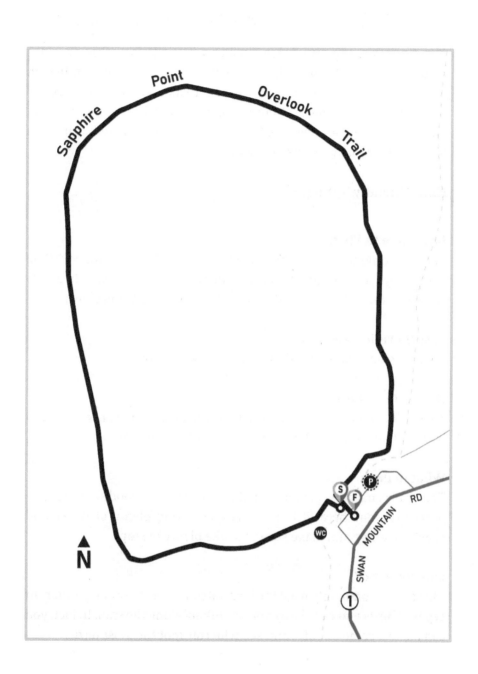

# MEADOW LOOP AND RIDGE TRAIL

The Meadow Loop and Ridge Trail is a 3.3-mile loop that provides fantastic views of Lake Dillon and the mountains surrounding it. Additionally, you'll see beautiful pine forests and have a chance for some of Colorado's most stunning photography. Part of the trail will take you through an open meadow and the other part will bring you high above the lake for the best views.

**Hike Difficulty Rating:** 3

**Best Time to Visit:**
The best time to visit the trail is from late spring to October. While there may be snow in the early summer, the leaves will begin to change in the fall and provide some of the most stunning views.

**Pass/Permit/Fees:**
There are no fees required to park and hike this trail.

**How to Get There:**
Take I-70 to Blue River Parkway in Silverthorne. Then, take exit 205 from I-70 and follow US-6 E towards Dillon, Colorado.

**What to Pack:**
This trail is partially paved, so make sure you have good shoes for any parts that may be a little more rugged. Bring plenty of water and snacks to enjoy and make sure you take plenty of stops.

**Can You Find?**
This trail is commonly used for birdwatching. See how many different types of birds you can see as you are hiking along the trail. In fact, you can make a game out of it and see who can spot the most birds.

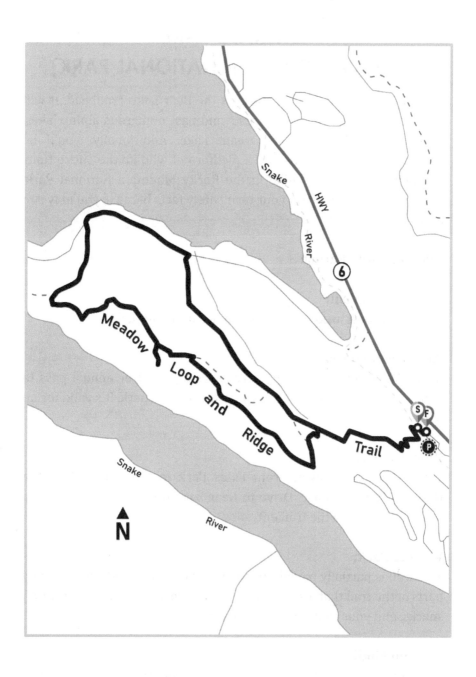

# EMERALD LAKE
# (ROCKY MOUNTAIN NATIONAL PARK)

This fantastic 3.2-mile trail starts at the Bear Lake Trailhead. It will bring you through tall pine forests and past numerous alpine lakes, such as Nymph Lake and Dream Lake. Additionally, you'll be surrounded by mountains and a plethora of wildlife the entire time. Whenever you plan to hike in the Rocky Mountain National Park, make sure to brush up on your bear safety facts because you may run into a bear or two.

**Hike Difficulty Rating:** 3

**Best Time to Visit:**
This trail is best used from mid-summer until mid-fall.

**Pass/Permit/Fees:**
Rocky Mountain National Park requires a permit or annual pass to enter. You will pay for this pass as you enter the park. It's valid for up to seven days.

**How to Get There:**
Take Highway 36 away from Estes Park to the Rocky Mountain National Park entrance. Drive to Bear Lake Rd. and take a left, then follow this road to the trail entrance.

**What to Pack:**
This trail is partially paved, so make sure to bring good shoes for any parts of the trail that are unpaved. Make sure to bring plenty of water, snacks, and your camera to take pictures.

**Can You Find?**
You can see many natural structures on this trail, such as Flattop Mountain, Hallett Peak, Glazer Gorge, and Tyndall Glacier. See if you can identify them.

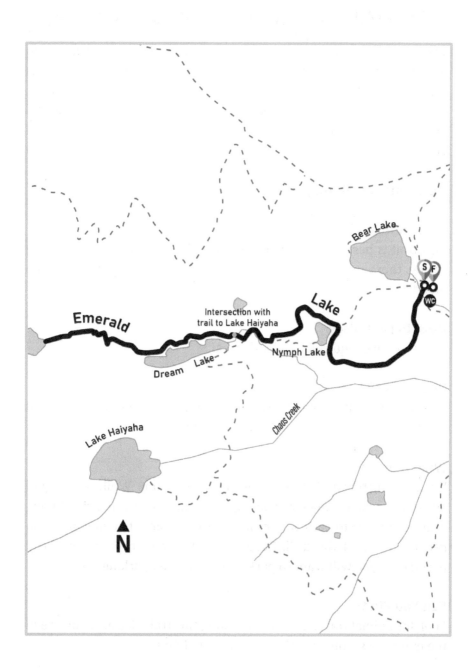

Emerald **Lake**

Bear Lake

Intersection with
trail to Lake Haiyaha

Nymph Lake

Dream Lake

Lake Haiyaha

Chaos Creek

N

S F

WC

# SAWMILL CREEK TRAIL (BRECKENRIDGE)

The Sawmill Creek Trail is located near Breckenridge. It's an easy loop trail that is good for all skill levels. Even though the start of the trail is rather steep, after you get over that one hill, the rest of the trail is flat. Many hikers report seeing wildlife along the trail as well as beautiful views of the lake at the top of the trail. This is a great hike if you are visiting Breckenridge.

**Hike Difficulty Rating:** 2

**Best Time to Visit:**
This trail is best used from spring through fall. However, during the spring, there may still be snow on the ground, and the trail may be muddy.

**Pass/Permit/Fees:**
No passes are required to hike this trail.

**How to Get There:**
The trail is located near Snowflake Trailhead at the intersection of Four O'Clock Rd. and Kings Crown Rd. in Breckenridge.

**What to Pack:**
When hiking this trail, regular shoes should be fine. While you should avoid flip flops or fancier shoes, you will not need expensive hiking gear. Make sure to pack water and plenty of snacks to enjoy once you get to the top of the trail. Keep in mind that there is no trailhead parking, so you will want to park in a designated parking area.

**Can You Find?**
Look for animal tracks as you hike along this trail. Because you are in the mountains, you never know what you'll find.

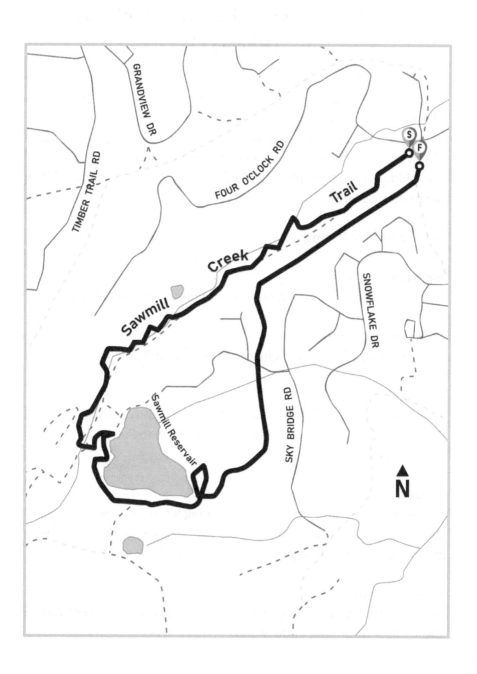

# LOWER CATARACT LAKE LOOP TRAIL (HEENEY)

The Lower Cataract Lake Loop Trail is a great place to hike if you're looking to spend an afternoon enjoying the scenery of the mountains. The trail is just under 2.5 miles long and features forests, lakes, wildlife, and plenty of wildflowers. Not only will you pass by many places that are popular for fishing, but there is also a waterfall near the middle of the trail. If you go in the summer, you'll be more likely to see intense falls.

**Hike Difficulty Rating:** 2

**Best Time to Visit:**
The best times to visit are from mid-summer to the end of fall.

**Pass/Permit/Fees:**
There is currently no fee required to park and hike the trail.

**How to Get There:**
From Denver, take I-70 W to CO-9 N towards Silverthorne. Take exit 205 from I-70 W and continue on CO-9 N. Drive to Forest Rd. 1725 to find the parking lot.

**What to Pack:**
There are two bathrooms near the parking lot, so you should be good for potty breaks. If you are interested in fishing, bring your fishing poles. Make sure to take plenty of breaks and drink water.

**Can You Find?**
Many hikers report seeing lots of ducks. See if you can spot any of these birds swimming in the water.

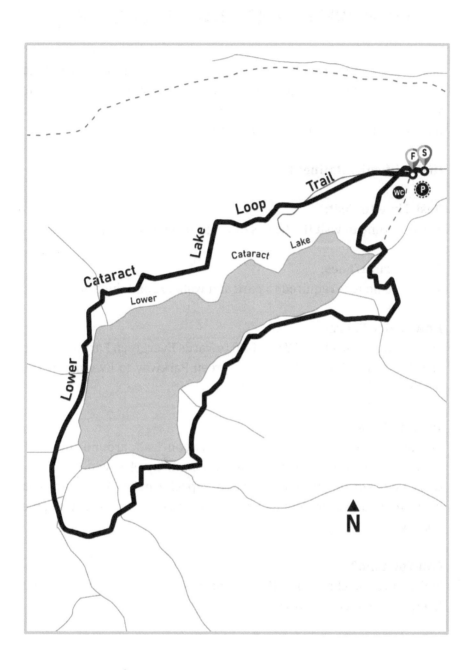

# EVERGREEN LAKE TRAIL (EVERGREEN)

The Evergreen Lake Trail is located in Evergreen. This gravel trail is incredibly family friendly. As you hike this 1.4-mile loop, you'll go around the lake and get beautiful views of the mountains and forests surrounding you. There are plenty of options for benches and picnic tables on the trail to stop and enjoy a picnic lunch.

**Hike Difficulty Rating:** 1

**Best Time to Visit:**
The best time to visit the trail is during spring through fall.

**Pass/Permit/Fees:**
There are no fees required to park and walk around the trail.

**How to Get There:**
From Denver, take US-6 W and I-70 towards Evergreen Parkway. Take exit 252 from I-70 and follow Evergreen Parkway to Evergreen. The trailhead is located next to the lake.

**What to Pack:**
You should be able to use a stroller as you walk around this trail. However, if you would rather opt for something else, you can either carry your small children or use a backpack carrier. Make sure you bring your camera to get pictures of your kids as they walk along the boardwalk.

**Can You Find?**
Make sure to check out the visitor center to learn more about Evergreen and Colorado's wildlife.

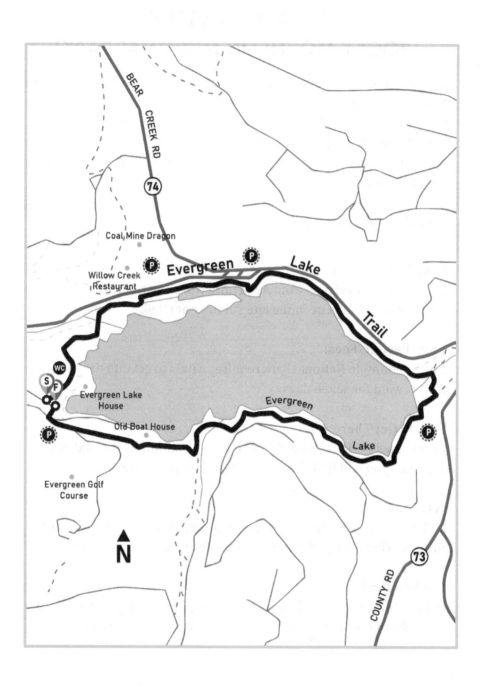

# DREAM LAKE TRAIL
# (ROCKY MOUNTAIN NATIONAL PARK)

Dream Lake Trail is a beautiful trail located in Rocky Mountain National Park. As you hike around the area, you will pass by numerous other lakes, such as Nymph Lake, before reaching Dream Lake. In fact, Dream Lake is aptly named. The waters of the lake are so clear that many hikers have reported being able to see cutthroat trout swim under the water.

**Hike Difficulty Rating:** 2

**Best Time to Visit:**
The best time to visit is from April until November. However, the best trail conditions will be in the late summer and fall.

**Pass/Permit/Fees:**
Rocky Mountain National Park requires a pass to get into the park. The pass is valid for seven days.

**How to Get There:**
From Estes Park, take US-36 W to Bear Lake Rd. At the end of Bear Lake Rd., you will find the trailhead to start your hike.

**What to Pack:**
Make sure you bring your camera to get some awesome pictures. Always bring plenty of water and snacks to enjoy along the way.

**Can You Find?**
In the summer, Nymph Lake is full of lily pads. See if you can find the lily pads on the lake as well as other wildflowers that are in the area.

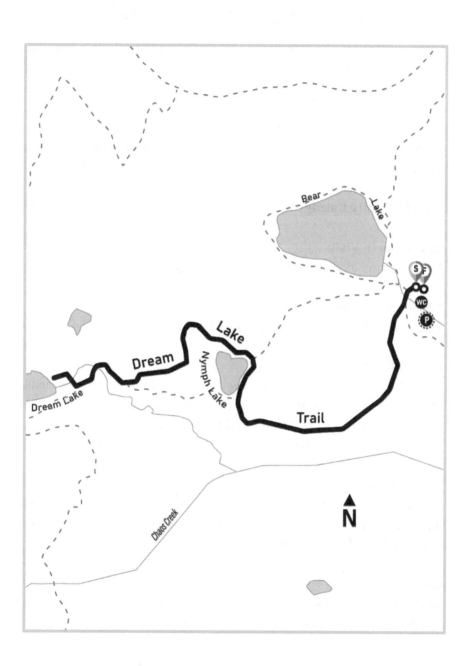

# LOST LAKE TRAIL (ELDORA)

Lost Lake Trail is a true treasure among Colorado trails. It is not easy to get to the trail, so you will need to have some hiking experience if you're going to attempt this one. However, you will not be disappointed as you hike four miles through forests and around lakes, view waterfalls, and enjoy the mountainous background. This trail is suitable for older children and will require some more rigorous hiking.

**Hike Difficulty Rating:** 4

**Best Time to Visit:**
The best time to visit the trail is during the summer and fall.

**Pass/Permit/Fees:**
There are no fees required to park and use the trail.

**How to Get There:**
To get to Lost Lake Trail, you will need to start at the Hessie Trailhead off County Road 130 near Eldora. Take the Hessie Trailhead to the Devil's Thumb Trail by taking Middle Boulder Creek to King Lake. Finally, you will follow Devil's Thumb Bypass to reach Lost Lake Trail.

**What to Pack:**
Because this is a longer trail, you may want to pack a lunch or at least bring enough snacks to get you through. Make sure you bring plenty of water and take breaks as needed.

**Can You Find?**
Moose are commonly seen along this trail. See if you can spot a moose or evidence that a moose has been in the area!

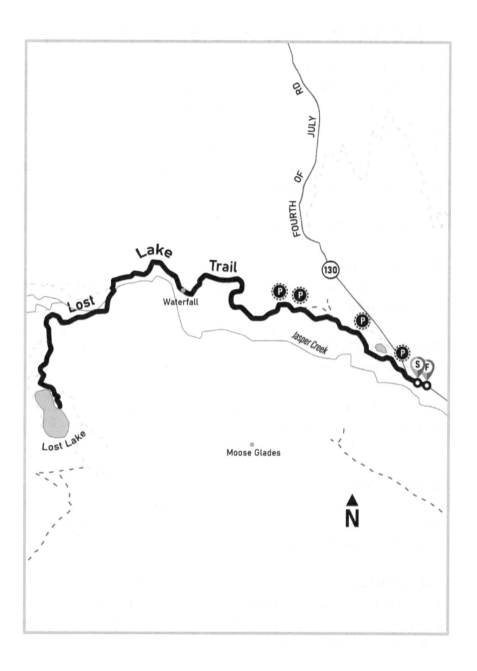

# MOHAWK LAKES HIKE (BRECKENRIDGE)

Mohawk Lakes Hike near Breckenridge is a six-mile round trip that brings you through forests, around lakes, and across creeks. It also has views of gorgeous waterfalls, mountainous backgrounds, and plenty of wildlife. If your family is used to hiking and is looking for a longer trail to enjoy on an afternoon, this may be the trail for you. Additionally, you can bring your fishing pole if you want to try fishing in some of Colorado's lakes and creeks.

**Hike Difficulty Rating:** 3.5

**Best Time to Visit:**
While the trail is open year round, the best time to hike is during the summer and fall.

**Pass/Permit/Fees:**
No fees or passes are required to park and hike.

**How to Get There:**
From Breckenridge, follow CO-9 S to Spruce Creek Rd. You will find the trailhead about 2.5 miles south of the end of town.

**What to Pack:**
Because this is a longer trail, you may want to pack a lunch and plenty of snacks. Make sure everyone has their own water bottle so that you are drinking enough water to stay hydrated.

**Can You Find?**
See if you can find an old mineshaft that is along the trail. It will look like an old cave and provides a great chance for you to experience some of Colorado's history.

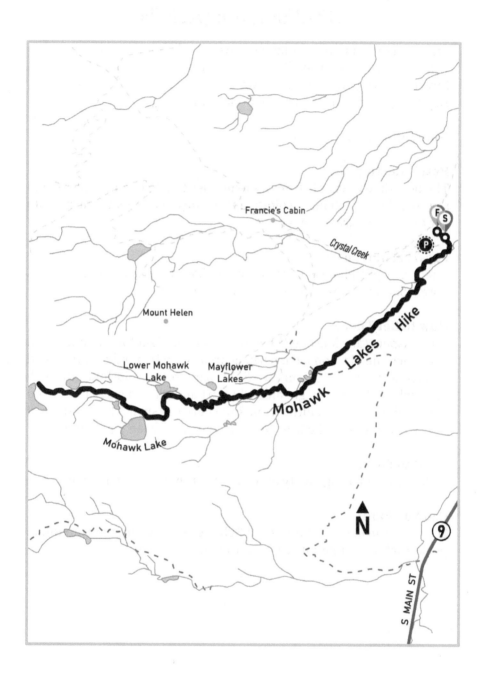

# CRATER LAKE (ASPEN)

Crater Lake is a popular hike near Aspen. As you hike the trails, you will get to see the Maroon Bells peaks as well as hike through beautiful forests before you arrive at Crater Lake. The trail itself is very rocky, so be prepared to do some mild bouldering.

**Hike Difficulty Rating:** 3

**Best Time to Visit:**
The best time to visit is from mid-summer to fall. If you would like to see the leaves change colors, make sure you visit during late September or early October.

**Pass/Permit/Fees:**
There is a permit that is required to hike in the area. Visit the U.S. Forest Service website to reserve your pass.

**How to Get There:**
From Aspen, take Maroon Creek Rd. and keep right for 9.5 miles until you reach the Maroon Lake parking area. Keep in mind that this road is closed from 8:30 a.m. to 5:00 p.m. from mid-June through September. Unless you get an early start and plan to stay all day, you will need to take the shuttle from Ruby Park in Aspen. This shuttle will take you directly to the trail and take you back when you're done.

**What to Pack:**
Make sure you bring plenty of water and a snack as you hike this trail.

**Can You Find?**
See if you can identify the Maroon Bells peaks. They are twin mountain peaks that are commonly climbed together.

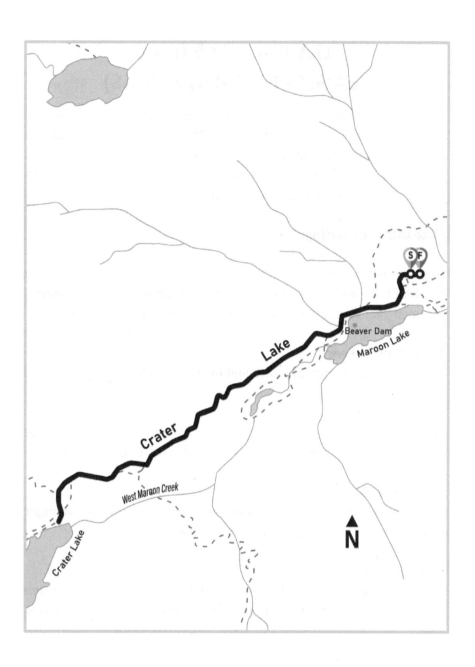

Beaver Dam

Maroon Lake

Lake

Crater

West Maroon Creek

Crater Lake

N

# LILY PAD LAKE TRAIL
# (EAGLES NEST WILDERNESS)

The Lily Pad Lake Trail is an easy trail that is good for all skill levels. While it is a little longer, the trailer itself is easy and provides plenty of areas to stop and take a break. As you hike the trail, you will pass by lakes, tall pine forests, and many small ponds. You will enjoy views of Lake Dillon as well as Buffalo Mountain.

**Hike Difficulty Rating:** 2.5

**Best Time to Visit:**
The best time to visit this trail is during the summer and fall. However, it's open year round if you and your family enjoy snowshoeing.

**Pass/Permit/Fees:**
There is no fee required to park and hike this trail.

**How to Get There:**
To get to the trail, take I-70 W to CO-9 N towards Silverthorne. Take exit 205 from I-70 W and drive to Ryan Gulch Rd. in Wildernest.

**What to Pack:**
Make sure you bring plenty of water and snacks. If you have younger children, make sure you take plenty of breaks.

**Can You Find?**
Several beaver ponds are located on the trail. See if you can find the signs that the beavers were in the area or maybe even see a beaver itself.

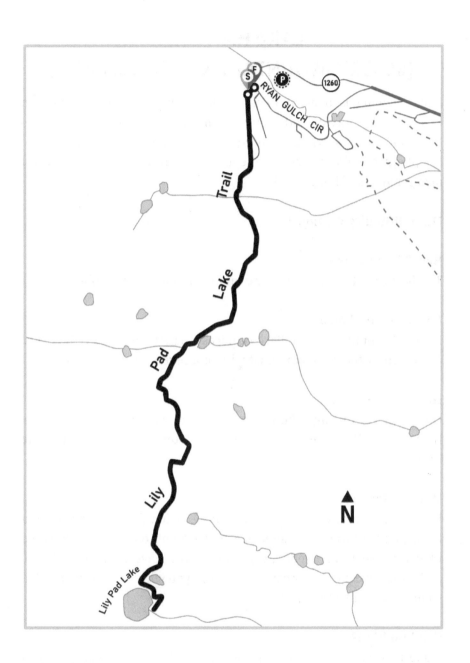

# LAKE HAIYAHA
# (ROCKY MOUNTAIN NATIONAL PARK)

Lake Haiyaha is a great destination if you enjoy hiking through beautiful pine forests and around numerous lakes. Before you get to Lake Haiyaha, you will pass by Nymph Lake and Dream Lakes. There are plenty of wildflowers to be seen during the summertime. You will also get views of Longs Peak.

**Hike Difficulty Rating:** 4

**Best Time to Visit:**
The best time to visit is from the middle of June until October.

**Pass/Permit/Fees:**
Rocky Mountain National Park requires a pass to hike any of its trails. As you enter the park, you must pay for a seven-day pass.

**How to Get There:**
Once you get through the Rocky Mountain National Park entrance, turn left on Bear Lake Rd. and follow it until you reach the Lake Trailhead.

**What to Pack:**
Because this trail does experience an elevation gain, make sure you bring plenty of water and snacks. You will want to make sure you take plenty of breaks as needed, especially if you have younger children. Make sure you pack your camera because you will see some incredible sights as you hike this trail.

**Can You Find?**
Make sure you look for animal tracks along the trail because plenty of wildlife is in the area.

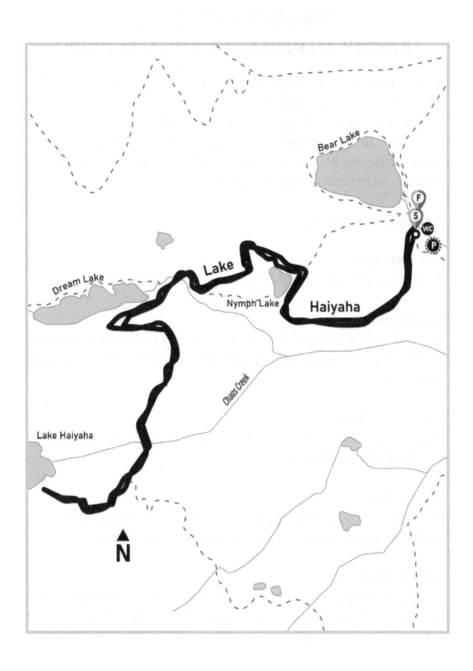

Bear Lake

F
S
WC
P

Dream Lake

Lake

Nymph Lake

Haiyaha

Lake Haiyaha

Chaos Creek

N

# SPRAGUE LAKE TRAIL
# (ROCKY MOUNTAIN NATIONAL PARK)

Sprague Lake Trail in Rocky Mountain National Park is a great trail for families with strollers and even wheelchairs. There is plenty to do around the area, but hiking the 0.8-mile loop trail near Estes Park is a great way to get outside and hike around the great outdoors. Additionally, you will have views of the surrounding mountains and have a chance to see incredible wildlife.

**Hike Difficulty Rating:** 1

**Best Time to Visit:**
The best time to visit is during the summer and fall.

**Pass/Permit/Fees:**
Rocky Mountain National Park requires a pass to enter the park and use all trails. Once you pay the fee for your car, the pass should be good for up to seven days.

**How to Get There:**
The trail is located on Bear Lake Rd. It's one mile west of the park-and-ride shuttle bus parking lot.

**What to Pack:**
This trail is stroller friendly, so feel free to pack a lunch and extra snacks. There are bathrooms and a parking lot in the area.

**Can You Find?**
At the end of the hike, there will be large boulders that many people like to climb. Even if you don't want to climb the boulders, you can still watch the people who do.

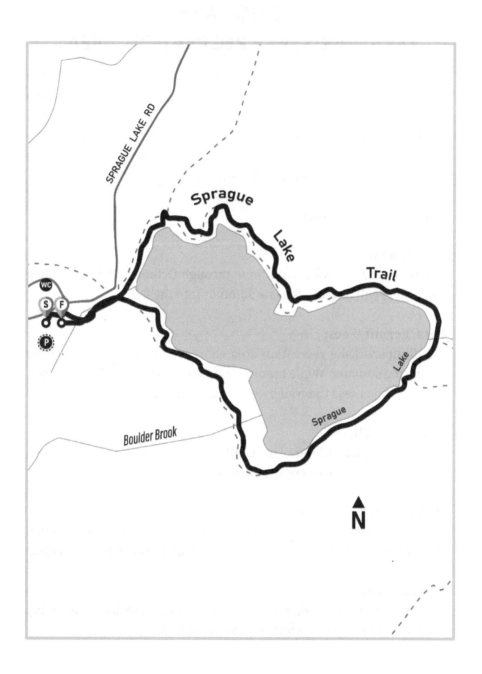

# LONG LAKE
# (BRAINARD LAKE RECREATION AREA)

The Long Lake Trail in Brainard Lake Recreation Area is a 1.8-mile out-and-back trail that is great for all skill levels. There is very little elevation gain on the trail, so it's suitable for young children and great for adults who do not want to break a sweat. As you hike through the trail, you will pass through forests, see rivers and plenty of wildflowers, and ultimately end at the lake.

**Hike Difficulty Rating:** 2

**Best Time to Visit:**
The best time to visit is from June through October. The best hiking conditions will be from the late summer into the fall.

**Pass/Permit/Fees:**
The Brainard Lake recreation area charges a fee of $12 per vehicle during the summer. While the area is closed during the fall and winter, you can still access the trail by hiking an extra half a mile.

**How to Get There:**
From Denver, take US-36 W to Lee Hill Dr. in Boulder County. Continue on Lee Hill Dr. until you reach the trailhead.

**What to Pack:**
There are bathrooms and parking near the trailhead that are open during the summer. Make sure you bring water and plenty of snacks.

**Can You Find?**
Look for the glaciers that can be seen through the tree line. Many hikers have reported seeing them as they hike!

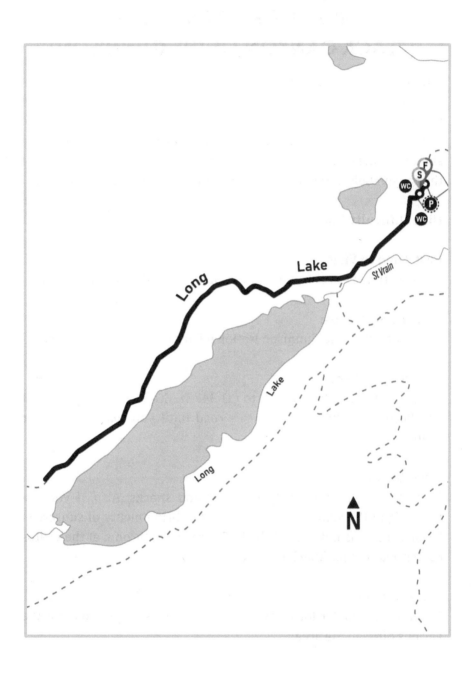

# RIM ROCK NATURE TRAIL
# (BLACK CANYON OF THE GUNNISON)

The Rim Rock Nature Trail near Black Canyon of the Gunnison is a great trail for an active family looking for a short adventure. Even though the Rim Rock Nature Trail is only 1.5 miles long, it does include some narrow passages. However, if you are an experienced hiker, you should be fine on this trail. As you hike, you will see gorgeous views of the canyon below and have the opportunity to see plenty of wildlife.

**Hike Difficulty Rating:** 3

**Best Time to Visit:**
The best time to visit is during the summer months through the fall.

**Pass/Permit/Fees:**
Black Canyon of the Gunnison National Park does charge a $25 fee.

**How to Get There:**
From Montrose, take US-50 E to CO-347 N. CO-347 N will turn right and become S. Rim Rd. Take this road until you reach the visitor center.

**What to Pack:**
Make sure you pack plenty of water and snacks. Also, if you are traveling in the summer, you will want to bring plenty of sunscreen because there is not a lot of shade. There is a bathroom at the visitor center near the parking lot.

**Can You Find?**
This area is popular for birdwatching, so make sure you look for the various birds in the area.

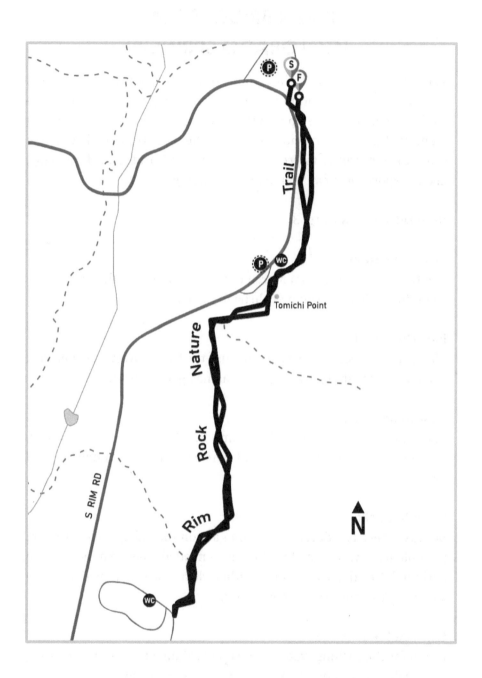

# SEVEN BRIDGES TRAIL (COLORADO SPRINGS)

The Seven Bridges Trail is a 3.5-mile out-and-back trail that features waterfalls, rivers, beautiful forests, and stunning views of Colorado's landscape. As you hike up into the canyon, you will see the stunning scenery of the land around you. One of the main reasons that people come to this trail is to cross the seven small bridges. Additionally, hikers report seeing an abundance of wildlife.

**Hike Difficulty Rating:** 3

**Best Time to Visit:**
The trail is available from March until November, but the best hiking conditions will be in summer through the fall.

**Pass/Permit/Fees:**
There is no fee required to park and use the trail. However, if you park in a non-designated parking area, you may get a $50 ticket.

**How to Get There:**
The trailhead is located on Gold Camp Rd. Once you get to this road, you will quickly reach the trailhead, which is marked by a sign for Trail 622.

**What to Pack:**
Because there is a decent elevation gain on this hike, make sure you pack plenty of water and take breaks as needed. Keep in mind that the parking lot to this trail is often either closed or overcrowded in the summer. Also, there are no bathrooms.

**Can You Find?**
Listen for the rushing water of the creek. Many hikers report hearing the creek from a ways away, so keep your ears on alert.

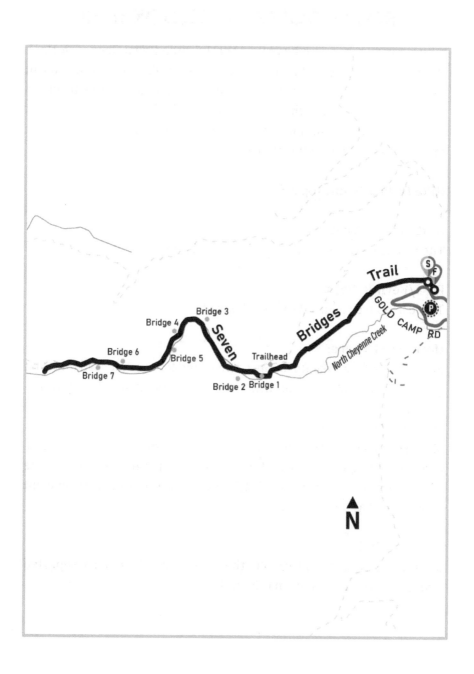

# ROYAL GORGE OVERLOOK TRAIL

Nearly every hiker who has hiked the 1.5-mile Royal Gorge Overlook Trail has raved about the views. As a trail for all skill levels, you can take your younger children for this short hike to see gorgeous views of the Royal Gorge and the scenery below. The Royal Gorge Overlook Trail is a great warmup for other hikes in the area as well as a great opportunity to take some fantastic pictures.

**Hike Difficulty Rating:** 2.5

**Best Time to Visit:**
The best time to visit is during the summer and fall.

**Pass/Permit/Fees:**
There is no fee required to hike the trail.

**How to Get There:**
From Cañon City, take Royal Gorge Blvd. and follow that road until you get to CO Road 3A. The trail will be on your right in about 3.5 miles.

**What to Pack:**
Make sure you pack plenty of water and snacks to enjoy along the trail. If you want to go to the Royal Gorge visitor center and bridge after the hike, make sure to grab some cash because there is an awesome gift shop as well as tasty treats.

**Can You Find?**
See if you can spot large cacti in the area. Many hikers have reported being able to see them from this trail.

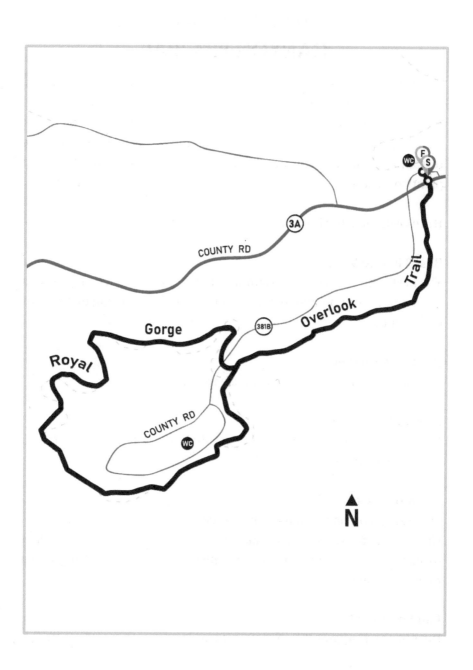

Royal Gorge

Overlook Trail

COUNTY RD

3A

381B

COUNTY RD

WC

WC

F
S

N

# ARKANSAS RIVER CANYON RIM TRAIL

The Arkansas River Canyon Rim Trail is a great trail for all skill levels. Even though it is a longer trail, there is very little elevation gain and the trail itself is clearly marked. As you hike the trail, you'll get amazing views of the canyon scenery and experience the unique terrain of Colorado. You will be able to see the Arkansas River and plenty of wildlife.

**Hike Difficulty Rating:** 3.5

**Best Time to Visit:**
The best time to visit is from summer to fall. However, it can get hot in the summer, so you may want to go in the early morning or towards the evening.

**Pass/Permit/Fees:**
No fees are required to park and use this trail.

**How to Get There:**
From Cañon City, take Royal Gorge Blvd. to CO Road 3A. After 3.5 miles, turn left on CO Road 381B.

**What to Pack:**
Make sure you pack plenty of sunscreen because there is not a lot of shade along the trail. Also, because this is a longer trail, you may want to pack a picnic lunch and have a plethora of snacks. Bring along plenty of water.

**Can You Find?**
Deer like to frequent this area. See if you can spot deer or their tracks.

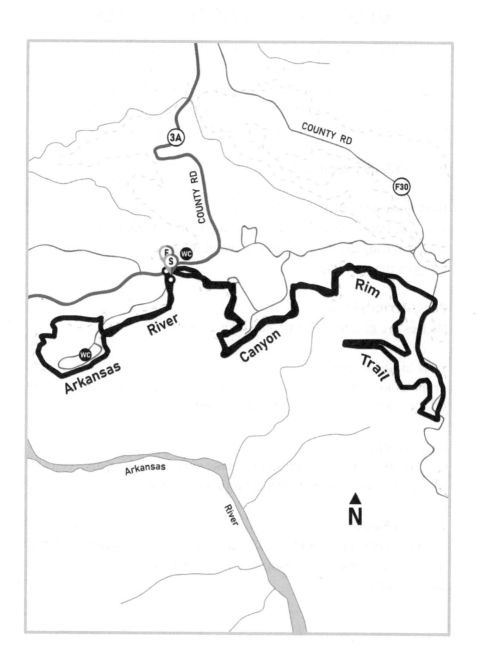

# FAR OUT AND CANON VISTA LOOP

The Far Out and Canon Vista Loop Trail is a great hike for all skill levels. The trail is well marked, and the 1.8 miles are filled with wildflowers and beautiful scenery that the entire family can enjoy. As you hike this trail, you will be able to see the eastern part of the Royal Gorge and stunning views of Pikes Peak in the distance.

**Hike Difficulty Rating:** 2

**Best Time to Visit:**
The best time to visit is during the summer and fall. However, it can get hot during the day, so you may want to go early in the morning or towards the evening.

**Pass/Permit/Fees:**
No fees are required to park and hike the trail.

**How to Get There:**
From Cañon City, take Royal Gorge Blvd. to CO Road 3A. Continue on CO Road 3A for 4.1 miles to CO Road 389B.

**What to Pack:**
Because there is not much shade, make sure you pack sunscreen and plenty of water. You may also want to pack snacks.

**Can You Find?**
While you may not want to find them, rattlesnakes are common in this area. If you hear a rattling sound as you're walking along the trail, stop and slowly move away.

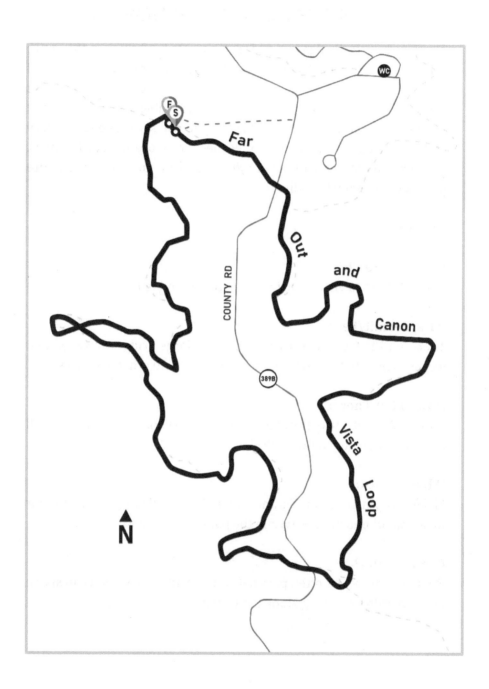

Far

Out

and

Canon

Vista

Loop

COUNTY RD

389B

WC

F
S

N

# ROYAL GORGE BRIDGE

The Royal Gorge Bridge is the largest suspension bridge in the entire United States. The bridge itself is wide and stroller friendly if you and your family want to cross on foot. Otherwise, there is a trolley that goes across the bridge if you are uncomfortable walking across it yourself. As you walk along the bridge, you will see gorgeous scenery of the gorge below and be able to see the Colorado landscape for miles. There are plenty of activities to do around the area, and the entire park is very family friendly.

**Hike Difficulty Rating:** 1

**Best Time to Visit:**
The best time to visit is during the summer and fall.

**Pass/Permit/Fees:**
There is a $25 fee to hike across the Royal Gorge Bridge. However, that fee gets you into the park and provides access to other activities.

**How to Get There:**
From Cañon City, take Royal Gorge Blvd. to CO Road 3A. That road will take you to the Royal Gorge Bridge.

**What to Pack:**
Make sure you bring snacks and water. There will be opportunities for food and other activities within the park if you choose.

**Can You Find?**
White water rafters often pass below the bridge. See if you can spot a group of rafters moving along the water.

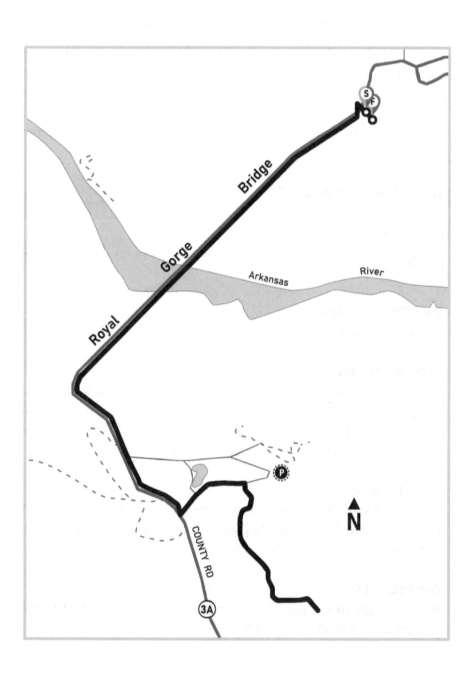

# MOUNT CUTLER TRAIL

Mount Cutler Trail is a short hike that takes you up to the top of the summit. From there, you'll have spectacular views of Cheyenne Creek and Cheyenne Canyon. The way up is a bit steep, but the views from the top are well worth it. As you hike up the trail, you will see beautiful wildflowers, an abundance of birds, and evidence of the wildlife in the area.

**Hike Difficulty Rating:** 2.5

**Best Time to Visit:**
The best time to visit is during the summer and fall for the best hiking conditions.

**Pass/Permit/Fees:**
There are no fees to park and use the trail.

**How to Get There:**
Take I-25 and exit at mile marker 140. Drive south and turn right onto Cheyenne Blvd. This road joins W. Cheyenne Canyon Rd. about 50 yards from the discovery center. Take a right on N. Cheyenne Canyon Rd. and drive for about 1.5 miles to the trailhead.

**What to Pack:**
There is little shade on this trail, so make sure you bring sunblock and plenty of water. There are also plenty of picnic tables along the trail, so you may want to pack a picnic lunch.

**Can You Find?**
When you get to the top, see if you can find the Seven Falls in the surrounding area. They should be visible below you!

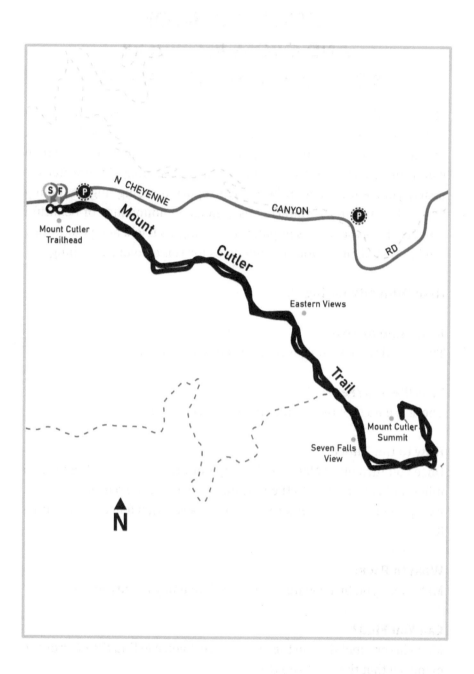

# FORSYTHE CANYON AND GROSS RESERVOIR (ROOSEVELT NATIONAL FOREST)

Many people like the Forsythe Canyon and Gross Reservoir for the spectacular views of the waterfall and reservoir. The Forsythe Creek follows a wooded and rocky canyon that creates many small waterfalls around the area. You can hear the rushing of the water for nearly your entire hike. Hikers have reported seeing huge bubbling pools of water at the waterfall as well as an abundance of beautiful scenery. The reservoir is popular for fishing, so if you and your family are interested, bring your fishing poles for some Colorado fishing.

**Hike Difficulty Rating:** 2.5

**Best Time to Visit:**
The best time to visit is during the summer and fall.

**Pass/Permit/Fees:**
There are no fees required to park and use the trail.

**How to Get There:**
Once you turn off of Magnolia Rd. and onto Highway 68, drive for two miles and turn right into the parking lot. To find the parking lot, look for a gravel area that has a restroom and a wooden fence surrounding it.

**What to Pack:**
Make sure you bring water and a snack to enjoy along the trail.

**Can You Find?**
Many hikers spot deer in the area, so see if you can find the deer or the evidence that they've been there.

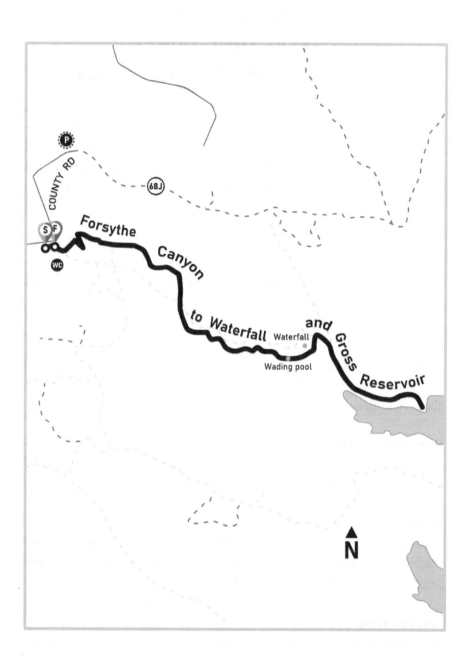

# SAND DUNES TRAIL LOOP (GREAT SAND DUNES NATIONAL PARK AND PRESERVE)

The Sand Dunes Trail Loop in the Great Sand Dunes National Park and Preserve is one that you won't want to miss. While hiking this five-mile loop trail near Mosca, you will see fantastic views of the sand dunes as well as Colorado's mountainous landscape. Additionally, this trail features a creek and some of the best birdwatching around.

**Hike Difficulty Rating:** 3

**Best Time to Visit:**
The best time to visit is during the summer and fall. This trail can experience high winds, so make sure to check the weather before you go.

**Pass/Permit/Fees:**
The park requires a $25 vehicle fee to enter. $45 annual passes are also available.

**How to Get There:**
From Denver, take I-25 S to I-25 BL S, then take exit 52. Follow US-160 W and SH 150 N towards the parking lot.

**What to Pack:**
Because it can get hot, make sure to bring plenty of sunscreen and water. Make sure to wear covered shoes to protect your feet and sunglasses because the sun can get intense.

**Can You Find?**
Many people will do this trail by horseback, so keep a lookout for horses in the distance.

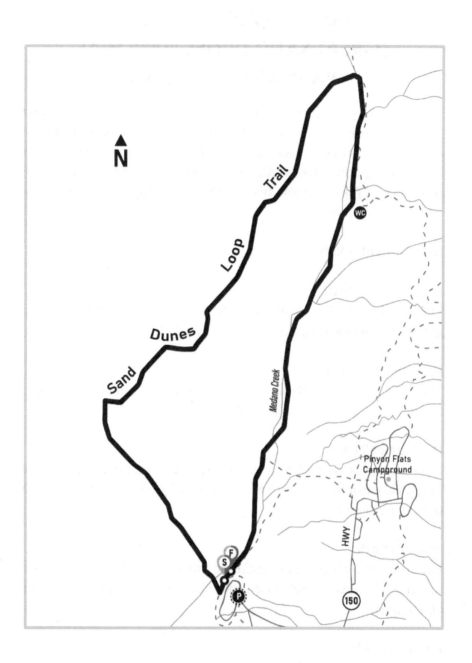

# DUNES OVERLOOK TRAIL (GREAT SAND DUNES NATIONAL PARK AND PRESERVE)

The Dunes Overlook Trail and Great Sand Dunes National Park and Preserve is an easier 2.7-mile out-and-back trail. It ends at a beautiful overlook that provides amazing views of Colorado's mountains and its breathtaking sand dunes. Along this trail, you will find beautiful wildflowers. There are also two benches at the top of the trail where you can sit to enjoy a snack.

**Hike Difficulty Rating:** 3

**Best Time to Visit:**
The best time to hike is from May until October. Because the winds can get intense in this area, make sure you check the weather.

**Pass/Permit/Fees:**
The Great Sand Dunes National Park charges a $25 vehicle fee to enter. $45 annual passes are also available.

**How to Get There:**
From Denver, take I-25 S to I-25 BL S, then continue for about 150 miles. Take exit 52 from I-25 S and follow US-160 W and SH 150 N to the campgrounds.

**What to Pack:**
Because there is little shade, make sure to pack plenty of sunscreen, a hat, and sunglasses. Wear closed-toed shoes and bring plenty of water and a snack.

**Can You Find?**
The top of this trail will lead to an overlook. See if you can spot the mountains and any wildlife crossing over the landscape.

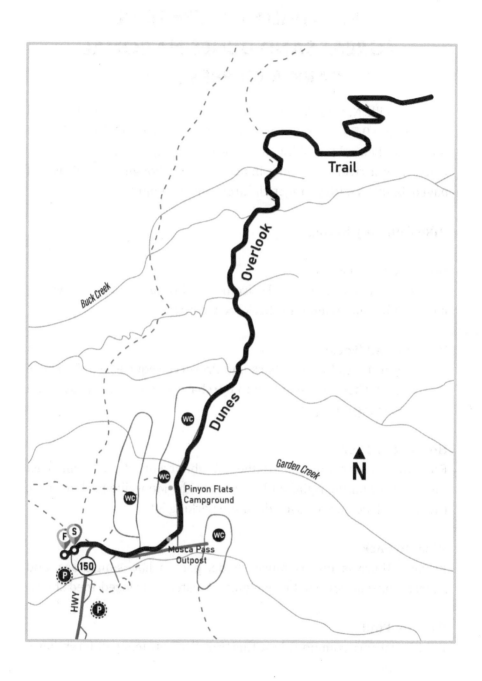

# MONTVILLE NATURE TRAIL (GREAT SAND DUNES NATIONAL PARK AND PRESERVE)

The Montville Nature Trail in the Great Sand Dunes National Park and Preserve is a 0.5-mile trail that is great for all skill levels. The trail itself is commonly used for hiking, walking, nature trips, and birdwatching. It features a river and some benches. Even though the trail is not paved, families with younger children can still enjoy.

**Hike Difficulty Rating:** 1.5

**Best Time to Visit:**
The best time to visit this trail is from May through October. However, it can get hot and windy, so check the weather.

**Pass/Permit/Fees:**
Great Sand Dunes National Park and Preserve requires a $25 vehicle fee to enter. There is the option to purchase a $45 annual pass if you plan on coming multiple days.

**How to Get There:**
From the visitor center, the trailhead is about a quarter of a mile past the entrance on the righthand side. From the Montville parking area, the trail will be on the east side of the parking lot.

**What to Pack:**
Because there is not as much shade, pack a hat, sunglasses, and sunscreen. Make sure to bring plenty of water and closed-toed shoes.

**Can You Find?**
Wildflowers are common along this trail. See how many different ones you can find.

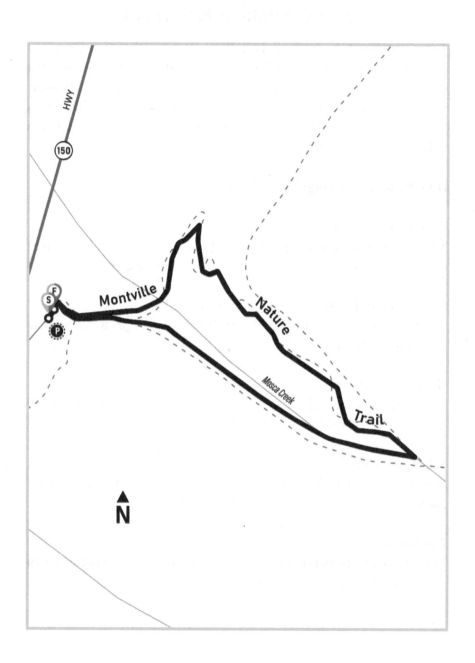

# SAND SHEET LOOP TRAIL

The Sand Sheet Loop Trail is a 0.4-mile hike that has gorgeous wildflowers and loops around Colorado's landscape. As you hike this trail, you will see the sand dunes and mountains in the distance. Commonly used for nature trips, birdwatching, and hiking, this trail is good for all skill levels. Make sure to keep an eye out for the wildflowers and wildlife!

**Hike Difficulty Rating:** 1.5

**Best Time to Visit:**
The best time to hike the trail is during the summer and fall. The area can get windy and hot, so check the weather before going.

**Pass/Permit/Fees:**
Great Sand Dunes National Park and Preserve charges a $25 vehicle fee to enter the park.

**How to Get There:**
From Denver, take I-25 S to I-25 BL S, then take exit 52. Follow US-160 W and SH 150 N towards the parking lot.

**What to Pack:**
Because there is little shade, bring sunscreen, hats, and sunglasses. Pack extra water and bring some snacks as well.

**Can You Find?**
This loop trail offers great views of the sand dunes, so make sure you stop and view them as you hike.

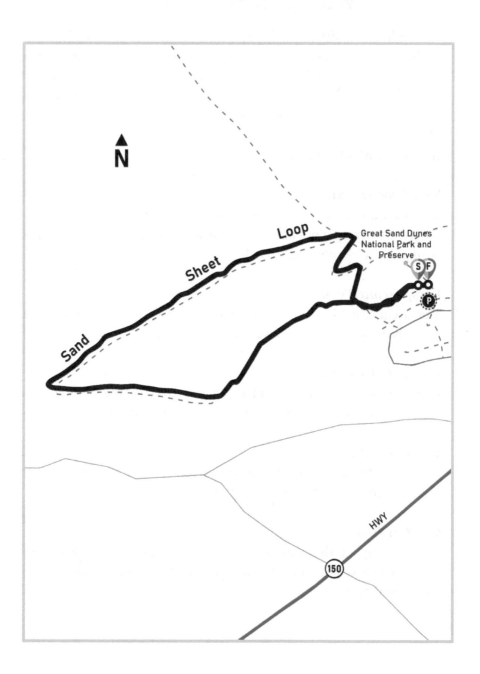

# WELLINGTON DITCH TRAIL

The Wellington Ditch Trail is a great hike for all skill levels. The hike itself is 1.8 miles and remains relatively flat throughout the entire trail. Used for mountain biking, hiking, nature trips, birdwatching, and running, this trail features amazing views of the sand dunes and has plenty of wildflowers along the trail.

**Hike Difficulty Rating:** 2.5

**Best Time to Visit:**
The best time to use this trail is during the summer and fall. However, the weather can get hot and there is little shade. The wind can also be strong, so check the weather before going.

**Pass/Permit/Fees:**
The Great Sand Dunes National Park requires a $25 entrance fee. There is an option to purchase a $45 annual pass.

**How to Get There:**
From the visitor center, head north end park in the Montville or Amphitheater parking areas. You will find the trailhead nearby.

**What to Pack:**
Make sure to pack hats, sunglasses, and sunscreen. You will want to wear closed-toed shoes and pack plenty of water and snacks.

**Can You Find?**
Coyotes frequent this area. If you are hiking at sunrise or sunset, you might be able to spot them in the distance. Don't worry, though. They will keep their distance.

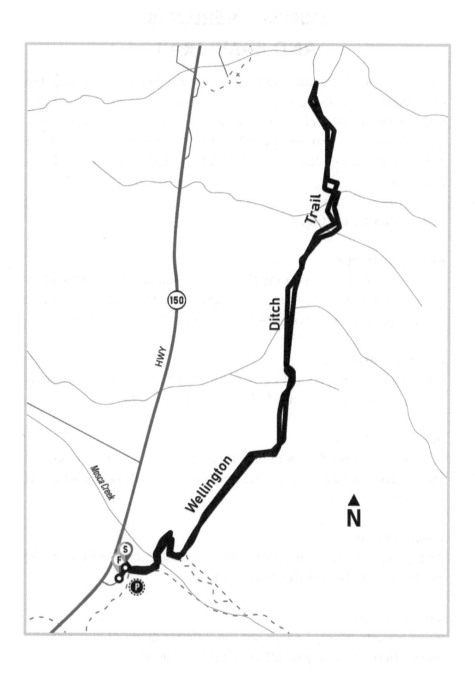

# DUNES OVERLOOK
# AND RAMP TRAIL

The Dunes Overlook and Ramp Trail will have you hiking through the sand dunes. Because it can be strenuous hiking through the sand, this trail is best for older children and those looking for a fun adventure. As you make your way along the 1.5-mile trail, you will have amazing views of the sand dunes and Colorado's sandy and mountainous landscape.

**Hike Difficulty Rating:** 3

**Best Time to Visit:**
The best time to visit is during the summer and fall, but it can get hot. To avoid the heat, it may be better to go in the morning or evening. It can also get very windy, so check the weather before you hike.

**Pass/Permit/Fees:**
Great Sand Dunes National Park requires a $25 entrance fee. There is also an option to purchase a $45 annual pass.

**How to Get There:**
From Denver, take I-25 S to I-25 BL S, then continue for about 150 miles. Take exit 52 from I-25 BL S and follow US-160 W and SH 150 N to the campgrounds.

**What to Pack:**
Pack plenty of sunscreen, hats, and sunglasses. Make sure to bring plenty of water because the trail gets hot.

**Can You Find?**
If you are into geology, check out the different types of minerals and rocks. There are plenty of different kinds in the area.

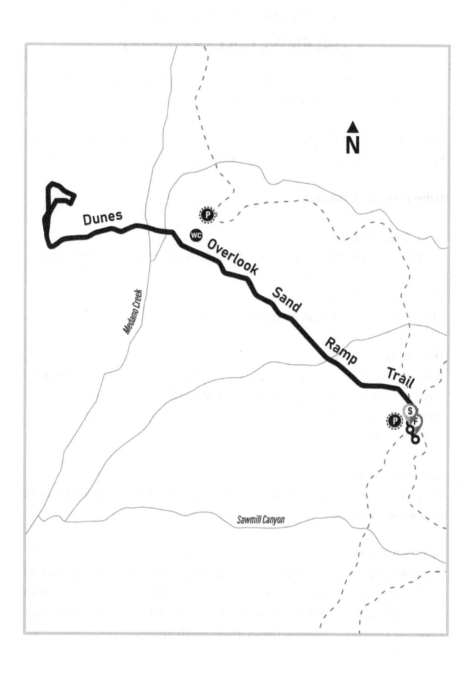

# DOC HOLLIDAY TRAIL
# (GLENWOOD SPRINGS)

The Doc Holliday Trail in Glenwood Springs will take you to a historic gravesite that marks the resting place of a famous outlaw. Doc Holliday, a notorious gambler and gunslinger, passed away in 1887 and made his final resting place in Glenwood Springs. Hike this trail for a historic trip into Colorado's history.

**Hike Difficulty Rating:** 2

**Best Time to Visit:**
Visit this trail in the summer and fall for the best hiking conditions.

**Pass/Permit/Fees:**
There are no fees required to hike this trail.

**How to Get There:**
If you are in Glenwood Springs, go south on Pine St. toward 6th St. Take a right, then take the 4th exit in the traffic circle. Take a slight left onto Grand Ave. and turn left for 13th St. Continue to Bennett Ave. to find the trailhead.

**What to Pack:**
Pack water and snacks. The trail is short but does experience mild elevation changes.

**Can You Find?**
The trail ends when you reach Doc Holliday's grave marker. At the end of the trail, see if you can find this historic gravesite. There are also plenty of markers that were commonly associated with Doc Holliday. Look for coins and playing cards along the trail.

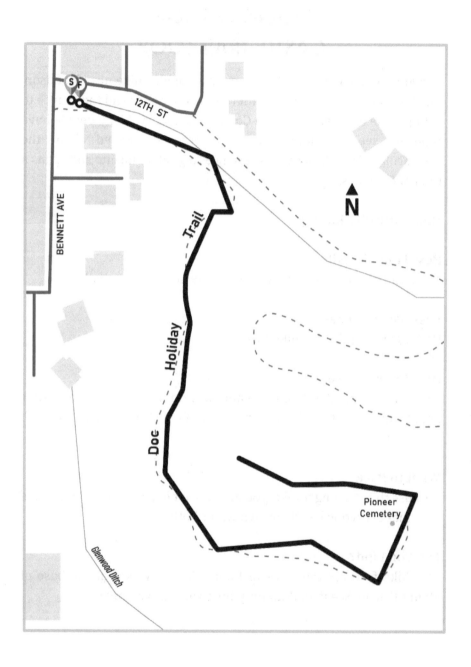

# MOUNT FALCON
# CASTLE TRAIL LOOP

The Mount Falcon Castle Trail Loop is a popular hike near Morrison. The hike itself features many different historic sites and the chance to get up close and personal with Colorado's history. Many people have reported seeing wildlife along the trail and raved about the spectacular views. The trail experiences a gradual incline and spans a total of 6.7 miles.

**Hike Difficulty Rating:** 4

**Best Time to Visit:**
The best time to visit this trail is from the late spring to fall.

**Pass/Permit/Fees:**
No fees are required to hike this trail.

**How to Get There:**
From Morrison, take Highway 8 and turn right onto Forest Ave. After about a quarter of a mile, turn right onto Vine St. The destination will be on your left.

**What to Pack:**
Because this is a longer hike, you might want to pack a lunch and make sure that everyone has their own water bottles.

**Can You Find?**
This hike features the ruins of John Brisben Walker at the base of Mount Falcon. See if you can find these ruins as you hike.

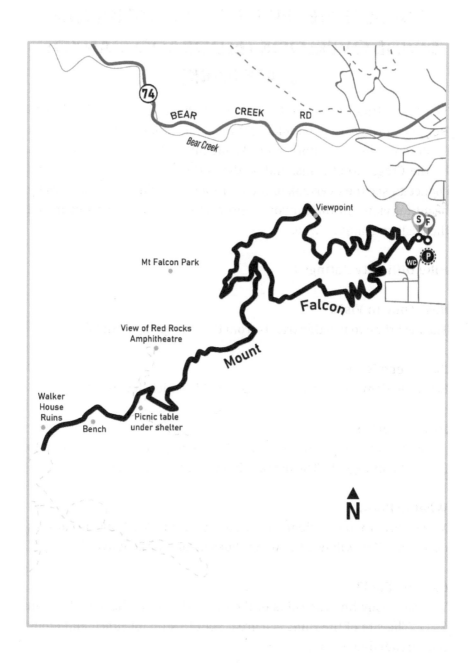

# CRAGS HOTEL RUINS AND CONTINENTAL DIVIDE OVERLOOK (ELDORADO CANYON STATE PARK)

The Crags Hotel Ruins and Continental Divide Overlook Trail in El Dorado Springs is a popular 2.9-mile hike that features some of Colorado's famous historic sites. While hiking the trail, you will pass by the Crags Hotel ruins, and at the end of the trail, you will get a chance to see the overlook of the Continental Divide. You will pass by beautiful views of the canyons below and have opportunities to see the Eastern Plains as well.

**Hike Difficulty Rating:** 3

**Best Time to Visit:**
The best time to use this trail is from the late spring until fall.

**Pass/Permit/Fees:**
Eldorado Canyon State Park charges a $10 vehicle fee to enter.

**How to Get There:**
From Boulder, take SH 93 S for five miles, then turn right onto Eldorado Springs Dr. The destination will be on your left.

**What to Pack:**
Make sure to pack plenty of water and snacks. Take breaks as necessary. You will want to wear shoes meant for activity.

**Can You Find?**
You can easily find the ruins of the Crags Hotel that burned down in 1912. The site of the ruins is a great spot to stop for lunch and enjoy the surrounding views.

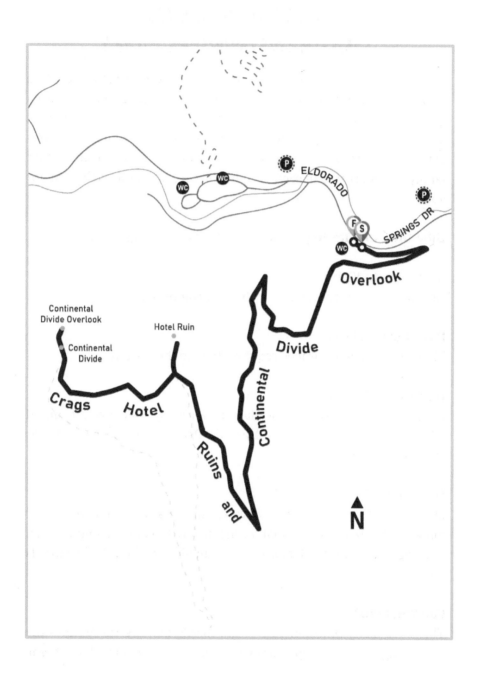

Continental
Divide Overlook

Continental
Divide

Hotel Ruin

ELDORADO

SPRINGS DR

Overlook

Divide

Continental

Crags

Hotel

Ruins and

N

# DINOSAUR RIDGE TRAIL
# (MATTHEWS/WINTERS PARK)

For the Dinosaur Ridge Trail in Matthews/Winters Park, there are two options. There is a paved road near Red Rocks that families can walk along to view fossils that are exposed in the rocks. However, there is also a four-mile out-and-back loop that is closer to Golden. The latter features numerous dinosaur prints and fossils. If you or any other family are interested in seeing prehistoric features, this is the trail for you.

**Hike Difficulty Rating:** 1.5 for short trail, 3 for longer trail

**Best Time to Visit:**
Hike in the summer and fall for the best conditions.

**Pass/Permit/Fees:**
There are no passes or fees required to hike these trails.

**How to Get There:**
From Denver, take US-6 W to Alameda Parkway. Take exit 2 from SH 470 E and turn right on W. Alameda Parkway. Look for signs for Dinosaur Ridge.

**What to Pack:**
Make sure to pack plenty of water and snacks. While there are markers that tell visitors what fossils they're looking at, it may be fun to bring a dinosaur book to see if you can identify the prints or fossils yourself.

**Can You Find?**
There are many dinosaur prints and fossils that are carved into the rock along the trail. Keep your eye out because there are a lot of them.

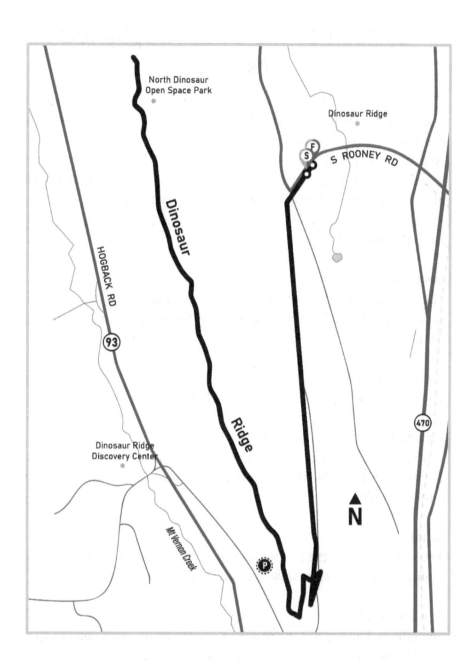

North Dinosaur
Open Space Park

Dinosaur Ridge

F

S

S ROONEY RD

Dinosaur

HOGBACK RD

93

Ridge

470

Dinosaur Ridge
Discovery Center

Mt Vernon Creek

P

N

# GARDEN OF THE GODS (COLORADO SPRINGS)

The Garden of the Gods in Colorado Springs features many different trails that vary in length and difficulty. From the visitor center, guests can take the paved trails that lead all the way to the unique rock structures that make up the Garden of the Gods. The main trail takes you directly up to the rock structures, but other trails will take you along a panoramic view of the stunning red rock structures.

**Hike Difficulty Rating:** 1

**Best Time to Visit:**
The best times to visit are during the summer and fall. Because there is no shade, the trail can get hot, so it may be best to go in the morning or the evening.

**Pass/Permit/Fees:**
There is no fee to park and hike to the Garden of the Gods.

**How to Get There:**
From Colorado Springs, take exit 146 off I-25 and go west for 2.5 miles. Turn left on 230th St. and you will find the visitor center on your left after one mile.

**What to Pack:**
The trails feature little shade and can get hot, so make sure you bring plenty of water, hats, sunglasses, and sunblock.

**Can You Find?**
Sometimes, bighorn sheep are seen along the trails. See if you can spot them if you go in the morning or at sunset.

# PALMER, BUCKSKIN CHARLIE, NIOBRARA, AND BRETAG TRAIL LOOP

The Palmer, Buckskin Charlie, Niobrara, and Bretag trails form a loop all the way around the Garden of the Gods. As you hike along this four-mile loop, you will see unique rock structures and have a full view of the Garden of the Gods. As you walk through the brush, you have a good chance of seeing some wildlife, such as deer or bighorn sheep. Because this is a longer trail, it may be best for elementary school children and older.

**Hike Difficulty Rating:** 3

**Best Time to Visit:**
The best time to visit is during the summer and fall. However, it can get hot, so it may be best to go in the morning or evening.

**Pass/Permit/Fees:**
There are no fees required to hike the Garden of the Gods trails.

**How to Get There:**
From Colorado Springs, take exit 146 off I-25 and go west for 2.5 miles. Turn left on 230th St. and you will find the visitor center on your left after one mile.

**What to Pack:**
Because the trail can get hot, make sure to pack plenty of water, hats, sunglasses, and sunblock. You may also want to pack a snack as this is a longer trail.

**Can You Find?**
Oftentimes, rock climbers will climb up the Garden of the Gods rock structures. See if you can spot some as you're hiking.

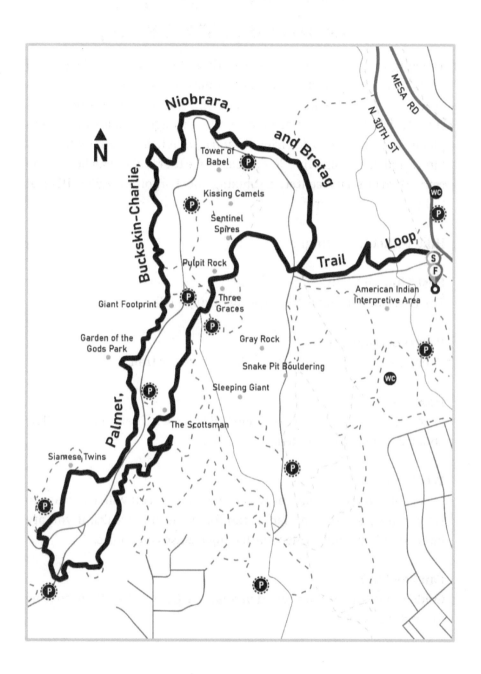

N

Niobrara,

and Bretag

MESA RD

N 30TH ST

Tower of
Babel

Kissing Camels

Sentinel
Spires

Buckskin-Charlie,

Pulpit Rock

Trail

Loop

WC

Giant Footprint

Three
Graces

American Indian
Interpretive Area

Garden of the
Gods Park

Gray Rock

Snake Pit Bouldering

WC

Palmer,

Sleeping Giant

The Scottsman

Siamese Twins

S
F

91

# FORGOTTEN VALLEY HIKE (GOLDEN GATE STATE PARK)

The Forgotten Valley Hike at Golden Gate State Park will take you 1.5 miles to an old homestead that still stands to this day. Plus, the ruins around the area are pretty neat. The entire trail is three miles from start to finish and goes around ponds, through woods, and across plains. The trail is also dog friendly and a great fishing spot for families interested in casting a line. For an easy hike that is about an hour away from Denver's city center, try hiking the Forgotten Valley Hike at Golden Gate State Park.

**Hike Difficulty Rating:** 3

**Best Time to Visit:**
The best time to visit is from spring through fall.

**Pass/Permit/Fees:**
There are no fees required to park and hike the trail.

**How to Get There:**
From Denver, take US-6 W to Drew Hill Drive Rd. The trailhead will be about 12 miles from Golden.

**What to Pack:**
Make sure to pack plenty of water and snacks. You will also want to wear proper shoes and plan ahead for bathroom breaks. If you are interested in fishing, bring your fishing licenses and poles.

**Can You Find?**
Golden eagles are often spotted in this area. Can you find them soaring through the sky?

# CLEAR CREEK TRAIL (GOLDEN)

Even though the Clear Creek Trail near Golden is 20.1 miles long in total, the part of the trail that is in Golden is completely paved and perfect for families with strollers. The trail goes follows a creek. Along the way, you will have a chance to see plenty of birds and wildflowers. There are many places to stop along the trail to go down by the water and cool off if you need.

**Hike Difficulty Rating:** 1

**Best Time to Visit:**
The trail is open year round, but the best time to visit is from the spring through fall. The trail can get very busy on weekends, so you may want to go during the week.

**Pass/Permit/Fees:**
Parking in downtown Golden is free.

**How to Get There:**
From Denver, take US-6 W and continue to the community of West Pleasant View. Take Johnson Rd. and Forward St. to 12th St. in Golden.

**What to Pack:**
Because this trail is so close to town, you can likely hike the trail without bringing a ton of snacks and gear. Make sure you bring water and shoes that are good for walking.

**Can You Find?**
This trail is right in downtown Golden. Because of that, the city of Golden has placed numerous statues along the trail. See how many you can find.

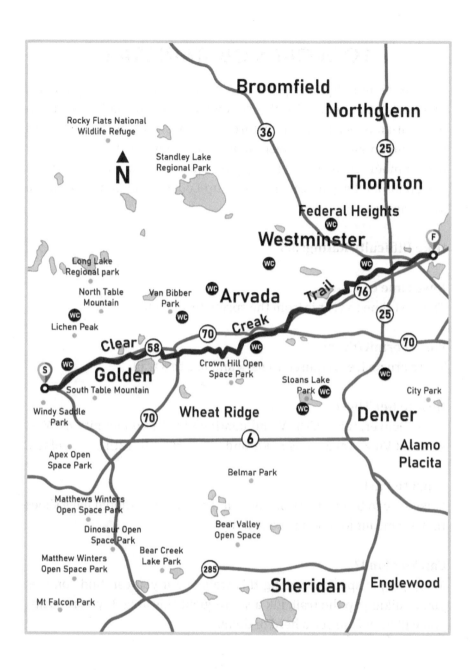

# LOOKOUT MOUNTAIN TRAIL

Lookout Mountain is a popular destination for those visiting Golden. The Lookout Mountain Trail, also known as Windy Saddle, is a 4.4-mile out-and-back trail that features gorgeous wildflowers and views of the mountains and Denver. Many who enjoy this trail will either hike or mountain bike up it to enjoy the spectacular scenery. If you are not up for a hike, you can also drive up Lookout Mountain to get the same views.

**Hike Difficulty Rating:** 3.5

**Best Time to Visit:**
The best time to visit is from the spring through fall.

**Pass/Permit/Fees:**
There are no fees required to park and use this trail.

**How to Get There:**
From Denver, take US-6 W and continue to the community of West Pleasant View. Take Johnson Rd. and Forward St. to 12th St. in Golden.

**What to Pack:**
Make sure to bring plenty of water and snacks. You should have shoes that are meant for hiking and activity.

**Can You Find?**
Many people spot deer along this trail. See if you can find some as you're hiking up the trail. Elk also frequent this area. If you're lucky, you will be able to see a herd of them.

# BEAR CREEK TRAIL
# (LAIR O' THE BEAR PARK)

Lair o' the Bear is commonly known as one of the best hiking spots for families. Not only is the drive into this area and canyon beautiful, but there are amazing hiking trails that are family friendly. One of these trails is the Bear Creek Trail. This trail is 1.6 miles long, features plenty of shade, and follows a bubbling creek. There are plenty of other trails in the area, so your family can stay all day and explore the canyons and creeks.

**Hike Difficulty Rating:** 2.5

**Best Time to Visit:**
The best time to visit is from the spring through fall.

**Pass/Permit/Fees:**
There are no fees required to park and use this trail.

**How to Get There:**
From Denver, take US-6 W and SH 470 E. Take exit 4 from SH 470 E. Follow Bear Creek Ave. to your destination.

**What to Pack:**
There are some awesome picnic areas around the trail, so make sure you pack plenty of snacks and even a picnic lunch. Bring plenty of water and shoes that are meant for hiking.

**Can You Find?**
The ecosystem in this area is very diverse. See if you can identify the trees and birds in the area.

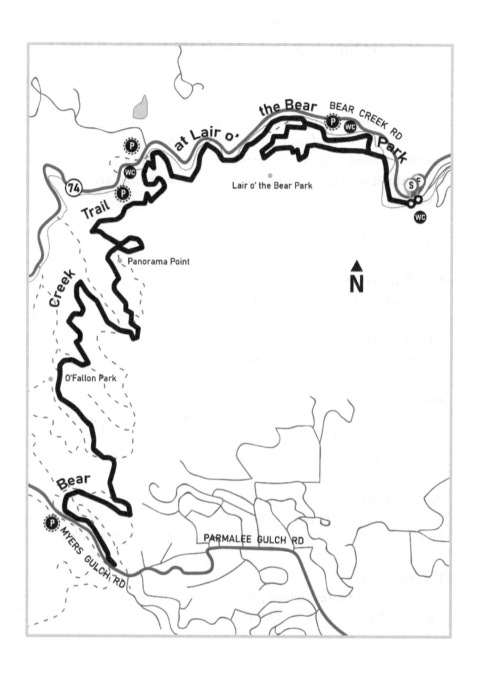

Bear Creek Trail at Lair o' the Bear Park

Lair o' the Bear Park

Panorama Point

O'Fallon Park

Bear

BEAR CREEK RD

Park

MYERS GULCH RD

PARMALEE GULCH RD

N

# RACCOON LOOP HIKE
# (GOLDEN GATE CANYON STATE PARK)

The Raccoon Loop Hike in Golden Gate Canyon State Park is a great family friendly trail that will take you through 3.4 miles of fields and forests. As you hike this trail, you will even get a view of Panorama Peak. You will also get the chance to go through aspen tree groves and meadows filled with wildflowers. In the fall, these groves turn a brilliant yellow and are some of the most incredible views in all of Colorado.

**Hike Difficulty Rating:** 3

**Best Time to Visit:**
The best time to visit is from spring through fall.

**Pass/Permit/Fees:**
There is a $9 self-service station fee to pay for parking.

**How to Get There:**
From Denver, take US-6 W and Golden Gate Canyon Rd. to Mountain Base Rd. Turn right onto Mountain Base Rd., and after three miles, turn left onto Gap Rd. Follow State Park Rd. to the trailhead.

**What to Pack:**
The trail is partially paved, but make sure to wear shoes meant for hiking. Pack plenty of water and snacks to enjoy along the hike.

**Can You Find?**
Along the trail, there is an old private cabin that you can see if you look carefully. Can you find the cabin?

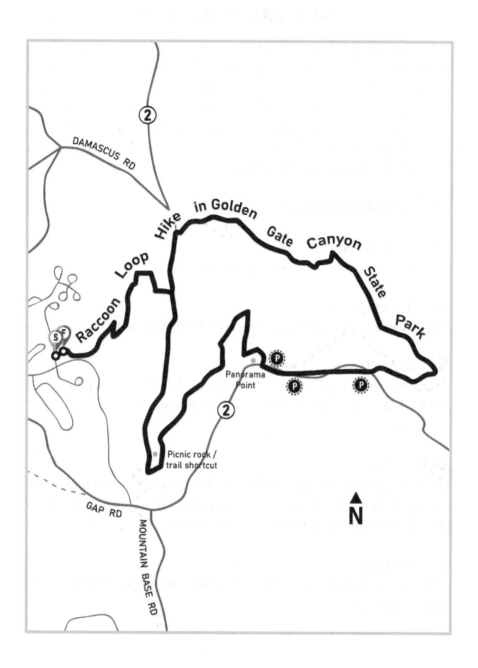

# PINE VALLEY RANCH

There are many hikes in Pine Valley Ranch Park. Not only are there hikes available for all skill levels, but families of young children can go to the area if they want to have a picnic lunch. Many of the hiking trails go along the river and through beautiful forests. Additionally, some hikes will take you out to Pine Lake for some of the best fishing near Denver. Furthermore, the 0.5-mile Narrow Gauge Trail will take you to granite cliffs that make for some great pictures.

**Hike Difficulty Rating:** 2.5

**Best Time to Visit:**
The trail is open from late spring through fall.

**Pass/Permit/Fees:**
There are no fees required to park and explore the area.

**How to Get There:**
From Denver, take I-25 N to I-70 W. Then, take exit 5A to highway 285 S and Jefferson County. Drive to Crystal Lake Rd. to reach your destination.

**What to Pack:**
Because there are so many hiking trails to explore, you should pack plenty of snacks and even a picnic lunch to enjoy as you hop from trail to trail. Bring plenty of water and your camera.

**Can You Find?**
There is a gazebo that is popular for picnic lunches. See if you can find it along the trail.

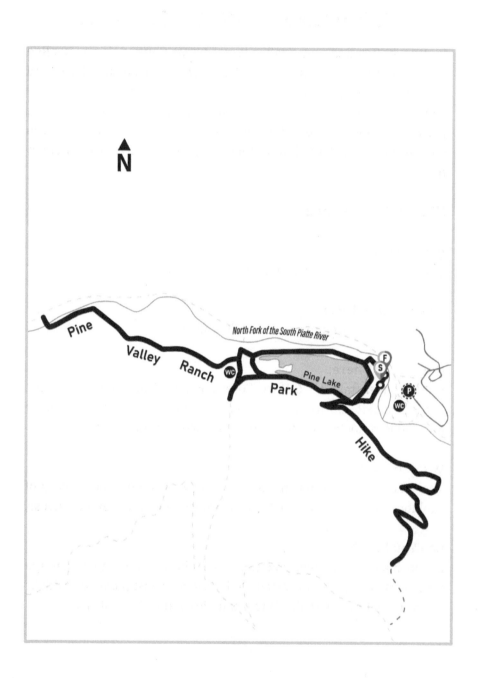

# RED ROCKS TRADING POST TRAIL

Red Rocks Trading Post Trail is located near Colorado's famous Red Rock Amphitheater. This trail will take you through the plains, and you will get spectacular views of the unique red rock structures that give the area its name. This trail is good for all skill levels and can be perfect for those interested in climbing some rocks. Additionally, you will get views of the Colorado foothills and a chance to see Denver from afar.

**Hike Difficulty Rating:** 2

**Best Time to Visit:**
The best time to hike is from spring through fall.

**Pass/Permit/Fees:**
No fees are required to park and hike this trail.

**How to Get There:**
From Denver, take US-6 W to County Road 93 in Jefferson County. Next, take exit 259 from I-70 W. Follow County Road 93, Hard Back Rd., and Red Rocks Park Rd. until you reach your destination.

**What to Pack:**
There is little shade on this hike, so make sure you pack plenty of sunblock, sunglasses, and hats. Also, bring plenty of water and snacks.

**Can You Find?**
If you hike far enough, you can reach the amphitheater near the staircases. If you are interested, Red Rock does host plenty of outdoor concerts that can be really fun for families and visitors of all ages.

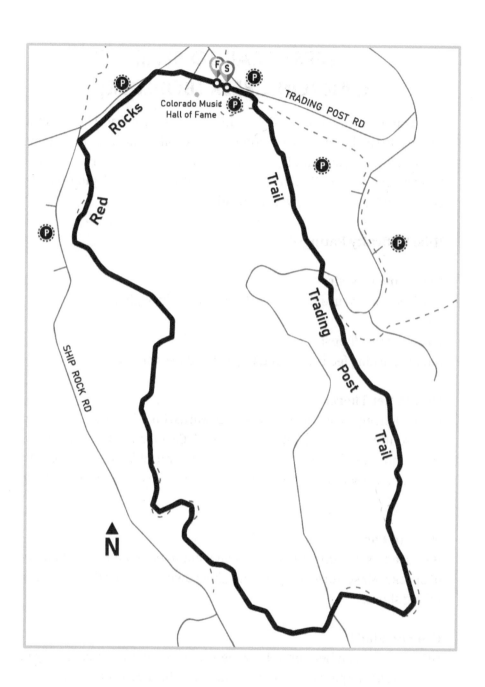

# MESA TRAIL TO BEAR CANYON CREEK (BOULDER)

This trail features some of Colorado's greatest scenery. The 8.4-mile round trip can be cut into either four- or six-mile trail loops depending on how much your family wants to hike. The Mesa Trail to Bear Canyon Creek near Boulder will take you by beautiful pine woods, creeks, and gorgeous flowering meadows.

**Hike Difficulty Rating:** 4

**Best Time to Visit:**
The best time to use this trail is from spring through fall.

**Pass/Permit/Fees:**
A daily parking fee is required to park and use this trail.

**How to Get There:**
From Denver, drive north on I-25 towards Boulder. Take McCaslin Blvd southwest. At the intersection of McCaslin and Marshall, take a right onto Marshall Rd. Next, take a left onto Eldorado Springs Dr. After about two miles, you'll find the south Mesa trailhead on your right.

**What to Pack:**
Because this is a longer hike, you will want to pack a lunch and plenty of snacks. Make sure everyone has their own water bottles and wear hiking shoes.

**Can You Find?**
Hikers have seen bear or at least signs of bears in the area. See if you can find skat or paw prints to indicate that a bear has been in the area.

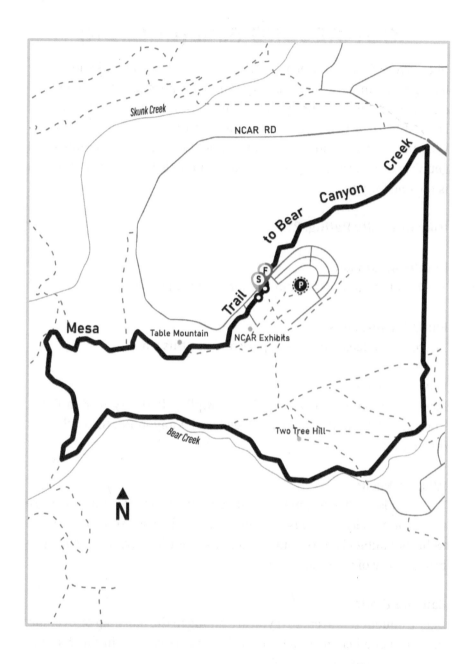

# COYOTE SONG TRAIL (LITTLETON)

The Coyote Song Trail near Littleton is a great family hike for those looking for an afternoon activity. The trail goes around a lake and offers beautiful views of the valleys and foothills in the area. This trail is good for nearly all skill levels and features beautiful wildflowers. Whether you are close to Denver and looking for a nature-filled getaway or you're simply looking for a fantastic family walk, this trail is the one for you.

**Hike Difficulty Rating:** 2

**Best Time to Visit:**
The best time to visit is from the spring through fall.

**Pass/Permit/Fees:**
There are no fees required to park and use this trail.

**How to Get There:**
From Littleton, take CO-470 W to S. Kipling Parkway in Ken Caryl. Turn onto W. Ute Ave. and W. Deer Creek Canyon Rd. to reach your destination.

**What to Pack:**
This trail is fairly easy, but you will still want to wear shoes that are made for activity. There is also no shade on the trail, so you will want to bring sunblock, hats, and sunglasses. Additionally, make sure you bring plenty of water and snacks.

**Can You Find?**
Deer frequent this area, so if you are hiking in the morning or evening, there is a good chance that you will see some grazing in the distance or even close to the trail itself.

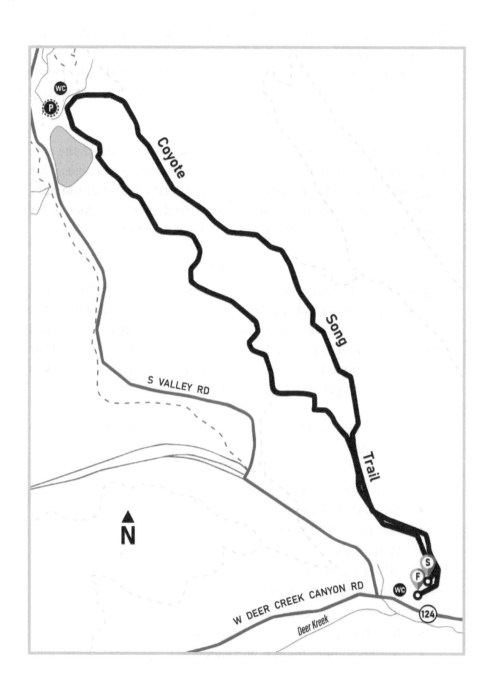

## Before You Hike

Now that you have learned about all the best trails in Colorado, it's time to start planning your hikes. However, there is plenty think about before you hit the trail. While some families can get away with simply hopping in the car and finding the best hike, families with small children will need to spend some time thinking ahead.

Depending on where you plan on hiking, you should research the area so that you're familiar with the surrounding amenities and hikes. That way, you will be fully prepared to have a fantastic hike. For example, you could look for the best places to grab lunch after your hike or for a local ice cream shop to reward yourselves for all the hard work.

## First Aid

As you plan your hike, it's best to bring some first aid equipment just in case someone falls and gets hurt. While no one wants to plan for the worst, you should absolutely bring bandages, pain relievers, and disinfectant wipes just in case. For most of these hikes, you will be near enough to populated areas, so if something does happen, you should be able to get help when you need it.

To create the perfect hiking first aid kit, you will want to have the following items:

- Antiseptic wipes
- Antibacterial ointment
- Bandages of all sizes
- Medical tape
- Blister treatments
- Pain relief medication
- Insect sting or bite treatment
- Non-stick pads
- Antihistamines for allergic reactions
- Tweezers
- Safety pins

- Multi-use tool
- First aid cards with phone numbers and family names

If you have all of these items included in your first aid kit, you will be ready to tackle any potential problems you encounter on the trail.

## Hiking Safety

When hiking, safety is a priority. That being said, make sure everyone has the proper gear and knows the rules of the trail. Even before you set out to hike, it's best to have a talk with your children about the importance of hiking safety, staying on the trail, and listening to adults.

This conversation can also include how to act when there are wild animals in the area and how to safely interact with nature. Speaking of wild animals, adults should brush up on their bear and mountain lion safety protocols for being out in the Colorado wilderness. While it is not necessarily common to come across these wild animals, it's best to be prepared so that you do not panic during an unexpected situation.

Additionally, you should talk to your children about what to do if someone were to get hurt on a hike. While parents anticipate and hope that this will never happen, it's best to have a plan in place just in case an adult gets hurt. For example, you can talk to your children about using your cellular device and trying to find another adult to help.

## Proper Planning

With this guide, you are well on your way to properly planning a hike. When you plan your hike, you should become very familiar with the area, memorize the trail maps, and bring plenty of water. Depending on the hike you choose, you will also want to bring snacks and even a lunch. For younger children, you should do your research and find a hike that best suits the needs of your family. Additionally, you should also plan potty breaks, when to get gas, and where to get food after you're done hiking.

The good news is that this guide has done most of his planning for you. Additionally, the more you hike with your children, the better you will get at planning. Not only will everyone learn their roles while hiking, but you will also know exactly what to expect as you're hiking with your family. You will learn exactly how much hiking your family can take and how to recognize when everyone needs a break. Even though this is a trial-and-error method, you can have fun along the way and enjoy the outdoors.

**Happy Hiking!**

We hope this guide has been helpful in planning your family friendly hikes. Now that you know everything you could possibly need to know about hiking in Colorado, we encourage you to enjoy the trails and keep track of your hiking experiences. As always, don't forget your camera as you enjoy all that Colorado has to offer.

27175401R00070